Microsoft Excel
for
Microeconomics

Microsoft Excel
for
Micconomics

MICHAEL I. DUKE
Blinn College

KATHERINE T. SMITH
Business Consultant

L. MURPHY SMITH
Texas A&M University

LAWRENCE C. SMITH, JR.
Louisiana Tech University

Editor-in-Chief: PJ Boardman
Executive Editor: Rod Banister
Managing Editor: Gladys Soto
Project Manager: Marie McHale
Editorial Assistant: Joy Golden
Cover Design: Christopher Kossa
Manager, Print Production: Christy Mahon
Production Editor & Buyer: Carol O'Rourke
Cover Printer: Phoenix Color Corp.
Printer/Binder: Courier, Bookmart Press

Credits and acknowledgments borrowed from other sources and reproduced, with permission, in this textbook appear on appropriate page within text.

Microsoft® and Windows® are registered trademarks of the Microsoft Corporation in the U.S.A. and other countries. Screen shots and icons reprinted with permission from the Microsoft Corporation. This book is not sponsored or endorsed by or affiliated with the Microsoft Corporation.

10 9 8 7 6 5 4 3 2 1
ISBN 0-13-142124-7

Microsoft Excel for Microeconomics

INTRODUCTION

The purpose of this book is to introduce students to the fundamental tools and techniques available in Microsoft Excel™ spreadsheet software. Applications are presented that pertain to specific microeconomic topics. Students will enhance their microeconomic analysis skills, while becoming proficient at Excel software. Students will learn through experience by following directions and creating example worksheets within each chapter. This book includes assignments for all types of microeconomic problems.

The book provides detailed instructions for using Microsoft Excel. These instructions are designed for the most current version of Excel but are sufficient for most other versions as well. Additional information is available on the Web site corresponding to this book.

WEB SITE

For updates, example files, suggested assignment schedules, and other helpful information, check the Web site (http://www.IOLBV.com/murphy/excel4econ).

NOTE: Microsoft and Excel are registered trademarks of Microsoft Corporation. All other brand and product names are trademarks or registered trademarks of their respective companies. Screen shots are used with permission of Microsoft Corporation.

DEDICATION

To the students who use this book. We hope each of you will enjoy the true success that is measured by moral character and personal integrity. Solomon wrote: "A good name is more desirable than great riches; to be esteemed is better than silver or gold" (Proverbs 22:1).

To our children: Hannah, Jacob, and Tracy. "Children are a gift from God; they are His reward" (Psalm 127:3).

KTS & LMS

To Doris Elaine Barfoot Smith, my beloved wife.

LCS

To my parents, Burton and Madeleine Duke (Exodus 20:12), and to my wife, Debby, the blessing of my life (Genesis 2:24).

MID

ACKNOWLEDGEMENTS

The authors are grateful for the contributions to this project made by Rod Bannister, Alana Bradley, Diane DeCastro, and Kristi Shuey. Additionally, the authors appreciate the support and encouragement they have received over the years from Milton Friedman, Jerry Hood, Ernie Moser, and James H. Packer III. We are thankful to Chris Osborne and Bruce C. Wood for their spiritual inspiration.

CONTENTS

Page

List of Worksheet Assignments   xi

1   *Computer Basics*   1
Components of the computer. Operating systems software.
Windows operating system. Loading your Excel spreadsheet program.
Saving files. Closing files. Retrieving files. Exiting. Printing.

2   *Making a Worksheet*   5
Spreadsheet organization. An illustration. Editing. Moving cell contents.
Inserting rows and columns. Deleting and shifting cells. Centering.
Changing column or row width. Copy and paste. Formulas. Writing
formulas. Copying formulas.

3   *Special Features*   12
Special features. Sorting words and numbers. Automatic sums.
Freeze panes. Importing data. Numeric formatting. Percentage symbol.
Currency style. Commas. Customized formatting. Functions.

4   *Charts and Worksheet Manipulation*   20
Line chart. Making the total revenue chart. Step one. Step two.
Step three. Step four. Making the P, MR, and PEC(D) chart.
Other types of charts.

5   *Data Manipulation*   26
Autofill. Data form. Data sort. Autofilter.

6   *Guidelines for Worksheet Design*   29
File identification area. Input area. Output area. Input alignment.
Manual recalculation. Testing.

7   *Step-by-Step Excel Example*   32
Creating an Excel worksheet. File identification and input area.
Output area. Creating a line chart.

Worksheet Assignments   39
Solutions to Selected Assignments   105
Index   144

LIST OF WORKSHEET ASSIGNMENTS BY TOPIC (Page 1 of 2)

Introduction to Economics	Perfect Competition
1. Real versus nominal prices*	26. Unit cost and revenue analysis*
2. Calculating real wage	27. Unit cost and revenue analysis
	28. Unit cost and revenue analysis
Supply and Demand	29. Unit cost and revenue analysis
3. Supply and demand*	30. Profit analysis*
4. Change in demand*	31. Profit analysis
5. Change in demand	32. Profit analysis
6. Change in supply	33. Profit analysis
7. Change in both demand and supply	34. Profit analysis
	35. Short run supply for the perfect
Elasticity	competitor*
8. Price elasticity of demand*	
9. Price elasticity of demand	**Market Efficiency**
10. Income elasticity of demand	36. Consumer and producer surplus
11. Income elasticity of demand	
12. Cross price elasticity of demand	**Public Goods and Taxes**
13. Cross price elasticity of demand	37. Impact of a tax
14. Price elasticity of supply	38. Impact of price elasticity on tax burden
15. Price elasticity of supply	39. Impact of price elasticity on tax burden
Consumer Choice	**Government Intervention**
16. Indifference curves*	40. Effect of minimum wage on the
17. Budget constraint	market for labor
18. Price change effect on budget	41. Impact of a price ceiling
constraint	
19. Utility analysis*	**Efficiency, Monopoly, and**
20. Utility analysis - deriving demand	**Monopolistic Competition**
	42. Economies of scale
Production and Cost	43. Monopolist unit revenue
21. Production function*	44. Monopolist profit*
22. Total and marginal product*	45. Impact of subsidy on profit
23. Production analysis	46. Monopolistic competition
24. Total cost analysis	long run equilibrium
25. Unit cost analysis	

* The solution to this assignment is included at the end of the book.

LIST OF WORKSHEET ASSIGNMENTS BY TOPIC (Page 2 of 2)

The Labor Market	Scarcity, Public Choice, and
47. Perfect competitor's marginal revenue product	**Public Policy**
	54. Production possibilities frontier curve*
48. Monopolist's marginal revenue product	55. Effect of technology on output using production possibilities frontier analysis
49. Labor demand and supply	56. Marginal analysis
50. Monopsony	57. Negative externality
	58. Positive externality
Investment Decision	
51. Present value*	**International Trade**
52. Future value	59. Impact of an import quota*
53. Investment decision	60. Impact of an import quota
	61. Impact of a tariff
	62. Impact of a tariff
	63. Foreign exchange rate
	64. Foreign exchange rate
	65. Comparative advantage*
	66. International comparative advantage

* The solution to this assignment is included at the end of the book.

ABOUT THE AUTHORS

Lawrence C. Smith, Jr.

Lawrence C. Smith, Jr., PhD is a Professor of Economics at Louisiana Tech University. He received his doctorate from the University of Mississippi. In his distinguished career, Dr. Smith has made significant academic contributions in teaching, research, and service. He has played many roles in various professional organizations, including serving 27 years as Secretary-Treasurer of the Academy of Economics and Finance. In 1999 he was selected as the first Fellow of the Academy of Economics and Finance. Dr. Smith's accomplishments include numerous professional journal articles, books, and professional meeting presentations. Among the journals in which he has published are: *Journal of Economic Education, Journal of Economics and Finance, Southwestern Economic Review, Journal of Real Estate Appraisal and Economics*, and *Oil, Gas & Energy Quarterly.*

L. Murphy Smith

Dr. L. Murphy Smith is a Professor in the Mays Business School at Texas A&M University. Dr. Smith's accomplishments include numerous professional journal articles, research grants, books, and professional meeting presentations in the U.S. and abroad. His major research interests are information technology, ethics, and international trade. His work has been cited in various news media, including *Fortune, USA Today*, and *The Wall Street Journal*. He serves on the editorial boards of several journals, including *Advances in International Accounting, Journal of Information Systems*, and *Teaching Business Ethics.*

Katherine Taken Smith

Dr. Katherine T. Smith has served on the faculties at the University of Mississippi and Louisiana Tech University. She has authored numerous professional journal articles and served on the editorial boards of five national journals. Dr. Smith has authored seven books, including *The Bottom Line is Betrayal* (http://www.iolbv.com/murphy/novels/), an educational novel that has been described as an "instructional thriller" and innovative way to present business concepts and issues to students.

Michael I. Duke

Michael I. Duke is a Professor of Economics at Blinn College. His teaching career goes back to 1978. Professor Duke has taught courses on economics principles, microeconomics, macroeconomics, comparative economic systems, and theory of leadership. From 1978 to 1981, he taught micro and macro economics at the United States Military Academy at West Point and served as the director of the Principles of Economics Course. He has published in *History of Political Economy*. He is a member of the Blinn Professional Association.

Computer Basics 1

This chapter briefly describes components of the personal computer, operating systems software, Windows, and starting your spreadsheet program.

☆ COMPONENTS OF THE COMPUTER ☆

As shown in Exhibit 1.1, the basic personal computer system consists of a monitor, keyboard, and a central processing unit (CPU). The CPU consists of three components: main memory, arithmetic logic unit, and supervisory control. Main memory includes random access memory (RAM) and read-only memory (ROM). The RAM of a typical personal computer varies from a few megabytes (MB) to over 500 MB.

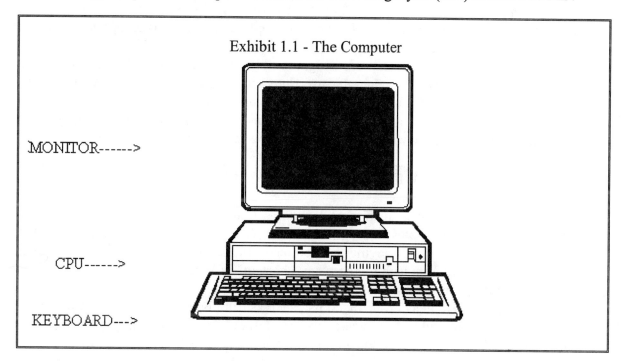

Exhibit 1.1 - The Computer

MONITOR------>

CPU------>

KEYBOARD--->

The box or chassis containing the CPU also contains other devices such as the graphics card which connects to the monitor, a parallel port which connects to a printer, a serial port which connects to a mouse, a modem or network card, a hard disk drive which provides secondary storage (typically ranging from four to over fifty gigabytes), a floppy disk drive, and a CD-ROM or CD-RW drive. The network card (e.g. Ethernet) enables a computer to be connected to a local area network or intranet, which then permits access to the Internet. The most widely used floppy disk drive is the 3.5 inch high density (HD) drive. The 3.5-inch HD disk can store 1.44 megabytes (MB) of data. A CD-ROM or CD-RW can store up to 640 MB of data.

The keyboard on your computer is made up of three basic sections: the function keys, the numeric keypad, and the alphanumeric keys. The alphanumeric keys, the main part of the keyboard, include letters, numbers, and a variety of symbols. The function keys, labeled F1 through F12, have different uses depending on the software currently in use.

The numeric pad is located on the right side of your keyboard. A significant key on the numeric pad is the NUM LOCK key, which is a toggle key that enables the user to switch between the number keys and the cursor control keys located on the numeric pad.

✶ OPERATING SYSTEMS SOFTWARE ✶

An operating system runs your computer and manages your computer's activities. The operating system of the personal computer functions much like the operating systems on a mainframe or minicomputer. For the IBM-compatible system, the most popular operating system is Microsoft's Windows. The Apple Macintosh has an operating system distinct from the IBM-compatible system.

Windows is a set of software programs that provides a graphical user interface. When running Windows, the computer user interacts with the computer visually and by use of a mouse rather than by solely typing commands. Two kinds of programs can be run under Windows -- the older DOS applications and Windows-specific applications that are designed to take advantage of Windows' special capabilities.

✶ WINDOWS OPERATING SYSTEM ✶

The most prominent feature of Windows is the use of icons (little pictures) to represent programs or groups of programs. After Windows is loaded (running), you run programs such as Excel by moving the pointer to the icon and double-clicking the left mouse button. A program icon represents a "shortcut" in Windows. Programs can also be accessed via the Start button on the lower menu-bar. By clicking on Start, you are given various options listed on a pop-up menu list, such as Run, Find, Settings, and Programs.

Microsoft periodically upgrades its Windows program. Windows uses "folders" and "shortcuts." A folder may contain several shortcuts (which access specific programs such as Excel or Word). Each folder has a menu bar that allows the creation of shortcuts or folders within that folder (select File - New).

✶ LOADING YOUR EXCEL SPREADSHEET PROGRAM ✶

Excel by Microsoft Corporation is the most widely used spreadsheet software. In order to start Excel, follow these steps:

1. In Windows, use your mouse to click on the "Start" button on the bottom left side of your computer screen. The button should expand into a box with several options for selection.

2. From the Start menu, select the Programs option, which will open another box with options. If Microsoft Excel is listed separately, double-click on the Excel option to open (run) the program. If there is not a separate listing for Microsoft Excel, then scroll to the Microsoft Office option and select Microsoft Excel.

OR

* If an Excel icon is shown on screen, simply double-click on that icon.

☆ BASIC COMMANDS ☆

SAVING FILES

A worksheet is saved like any other file by using the following commands:

1. Choose "File" in the Excel top menu bar and select the Save-As option.
2. The Save-As menu box will appear and the name "Book1.xls" will be highlighted in the file name box. "Book1" is simply the default name Excel uses and "xls" is the filename extension of an Excel worksheet. You can replace "Book1" with a new filename; we recommend keeping the "xls" extension so that you know it is an Excel worksheet.
3. Now that you have named the worksheet, you can save it in the future by simply clicking on the Save icon (picture of a floppy disk).

CLOSING FILES

Similar to other files, a worksheet is closed by simply clicking on the "X" button in the upper right-hand corner of the menu bar.

RETRIEVING FILES

A worksheet is retrieved like any file by using the following commands:

1. Click on the "Open" icon (picture of an open folder).
2. An Open File box will appear with a list of files or folders. Double-click on the file you want opened. Note: If the file is not listed, then you are in the wrong folder. Access the correct folder by clicking on the arrow within the "Looking in" box at the top. A list of folders or directories will appear for your choosing.

EXITING

The Excel program can be exited like any other program by clicking on the "X" button in the upper right-hand corner of the screen (this appears above the "X" button used for closing the worksheet).

PRINTING

Using the print command, the entire worksheet can be printed or just sections of it. For printing sections of your worksheet, first highlight the section you want printed and then click on File in the menu bar. Select Print. Under the print options, choose Selection. Another very useful step is to select File - Print Preview to see how your output will look.

Making a Worksheet 2

☐ SPREADSHEET ORGANIZATION ☐

Once the spreadsheet software is loaded, a screen appears similar to Exhibit 2.1. The spreadsheet you see is called a worksheet in Excel.

Exhibit 2.1 - Basic Excel Worksheet

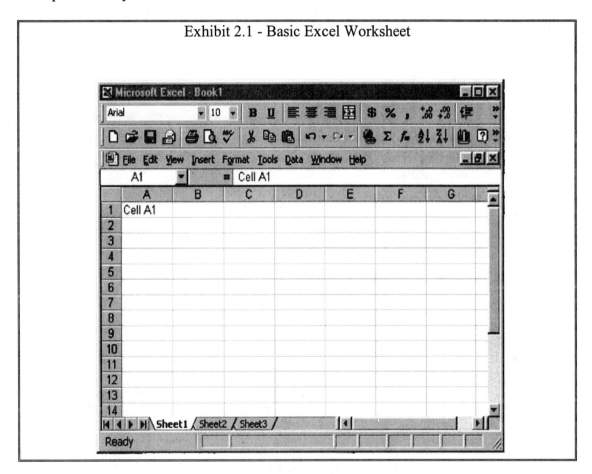

The letters across the top of a worksheet correspond to columns. The numbers along the left side of a worksheet correspond to rows. The box at the intersection of a column and row is referred to as the cell location. Cells are where data, either text or mathematical expressions, are entered. In Exhibit 2.1, the words "Cell A1" have been typed into cell A1. Directly above the cell is the control panel that shows the cell designation, in this case it is A1. To the right of that, next to an equal sign, you'll notice another panel containing "Cell A1." When a cell is clicked upon, its contents automatically appear in this panel.

Each Excel file, called a workbook, can hold several worksheets. Worksheets are saved, closed and printed like any other file, by first clicking on the "File" selection in the top menu bar or by clicking on the appropriate icons at the top of the worksheet currently in use.

☐   AN ILLUSTRATION   ☐

To begin your familiarization with Excel worksheets, we will create a worksheet using just the essential commands. Step-by-step instructions to accomplish these commands will be provided.

Assume, as an economist, your boss has requested that you show the relationship between the price, quantity demanded, and quantity supplied of your firm's product, toy robots. A market survey was used to determine the quantity demanded (QD) at different prices. The relationship proved to be linear with the equation: QD = 10 - .1*P.   In preparation for the analysis, we will first create a worksheet using the information below. (Quantity supplied will be added later.)

Toy Robot	
Price	QD
0	10
20	8
40	6
60	4
80	2
100	0

To start, click on cell A1 with your mouse and type in "Toy Robot." When finished typing, press Enter or click on another cell; the typed data will automatically be inserted into the worksheet. Now click on cell A2 and type in "Price." Another way to move among the cells is to use the arrow keys. Beginning with cell A3, proceed to type the amounts into individual cells below Price. To make the worksheet easier to read, we'll skip a column and type "QD" into cell C2. Type the quantities into the cells below QD. Exhibit 2.2 shows how your worksheet will appear.

Note that Excel automatically right-justifies a number after it is entered into a cell. If you make a mistake in typing the numbers, the ensuing section on editing will show how to correct it.

Exhibit 2.2 - Robot Worksheet

	A	B	C
1	Toy Robot		
2	Price		QD
3	0		10
4	20		8
5	40		6
6	60		4
7	80		2
8	100		0

☐ EDITING ☐

A cell can be put into edit mode by double clicking on the cell. Excel will then allow you to move around within the cell and change the contents. If you want to replace the entire contents of a cell, simply click on the cell once and type in the new contents. If you want to delete the entire contents of a cell, click on the cell and press the delete key.

As noted earlier, when a cell is clicked upon, its contents automatically enter the panel at the top of the worksheet next to the equal sign. Another way to edit a cell is to place your cursor within this panel and type.

MOVING CELL CONTENTS

Our worksheet would look better if "Toy Robot" was placed between the price and QD columns. To move "Toy Robot" to cell B1:

1. Click on the cell you wish to move (A1).
2. Position the pointer on the bottom right corner of the cell until the pointer turns into a white arrow. Hold down the left mouse button and drag the pointer to the new cell. Release the mouse button, and the contents will appear in the new cell.

To move a block of cells, highlight the cells by holding down the left mouse button and then move the entire block at once by dragging the cursor to the desired location.

INSERTING ROWS AND COLUMNS

Referring to our robot worksheet, suppose the boss wants to see the quantity demanded for every multiple of $10 up to $100. A row can be inserted as follows:

1.   Rows are added **above** the cell pointer, so position your cell pointer accordingly. In our example, to add 10 to the list of prices, click on cell A4 (which currently contains "20").
2.   Select the Insert menu and choose Row to insert.

Add rows to your robot worksheet and fill in the prices and quantity demanded as shown in Exhibit 2.3.

Columns may also be inserted into a worksheet. Columns are added to the **left** of the pointer by choosing the Insert - Column.

Exhibit 2.3 - Robot Worksheet			
	Toy Robot		
Price		QD	
0		10	
10		9	
20		8	
30		7	
40		6	
50		5	
60		4	
70		3	
80		2	
90		1	
100		0	

DELETING AND SHIFTING CELLS

As previously discussed, clicking on the cell and pressing the delete key can remove the contents of a cell. However, assume we want to remove the entire row containing "0" in the price column without leaving an empty row. This is accomplished by deleting the unwanted row and shifting the remaining rows up. In regards to the robot worksheet, use the following commands:

1.   Click on the cell that contains "0."
2.   Select the Edit menu and choose the Delete option.
3.   Excel gives you the option of deleting the entire row; click on that option. For rows, cells are shifted up.

If an entire column is deleted, columns will be shifted to the left. A single cell within a column or row can also be deleted and the remaining cells within the column/row will be shifted.

CENTERING

Data within a single cell can be centered by clicking on the cell and then clicking on the icon that displays centered lines. The icon is found on the top toolbar.

Let's improve the looks of the robot worksheet by centering both of the columns. Using the left mouse button, highlight the entire price column including its title, then click on the icon with centered lines. Do this for the quantity-demanded column also.

Suppose we need a different heading on the worksheet. Delete "Toy Robot." Retype "Wacky Toy Robots by Robots-R-Us" into cell A1. The heading will run over into the adjacent empty cells. Press enter to leave the edit mode.

We'll center the new heading between columns A and E to allow space for a quantity supplied (QS) column that will be added later. Highlight row 1 from A to E. Then click on the icon with the boxed in "a" (merge and center icon). Your worksheet should now resemble Exhibit 2.4.

Exhibit 2.4 - Robot Worksheet				
Wacky Toy Robots by Robots-R-Us				
Price		QD		QS
10		9		
20		8		
30		7		
40		6		
50		5		
60		4		
70		3		
80		2		
90		1		
100		0		

CHANGING COLUMN OR ROW WIDTH

When the spreadsheet program is first loaded, the column width will be eight characters. If your cell data exceeds the cell width, the data will simply run into the adjacent empty cell. However, if the adjacent cell is not empty, the overflow data will be truncated at the cell border.

Columns can be made wider or smaller. Position the cursor at the top of the screen on the boundary line between the lettered column headings (e.g. the line between A and B). The cursor should change into a "+." Click-and-drag using the left mouse key; hold it while "dragging" the column to a different width. Row width can be changed by positioning the cursor between the row numbers on the left. Note: you must be out of the edit mode in order to change width or height.

COPY AND PASTE

The Copy and Paste commands enable you to move and duplicate the contents of one cell or cells to another cell or cells within the worksheet. Anything already in the receiving cell will be deleted. These commands work using the icons as you would on any other file. Note that a cell must be highlighted before you can copy.

Cells or entire worksheets can be copied and pasted into other documents using the copy and paste icons. Here are two useful paste options that new Excel versions offer:

1. Select the Edit menu. Choose Paste Special.
2. It will give you several options as to how to paste.
   a. The "Microsoft Excel Worksheet" option allows you to paste a worksheet into a document (e.g. a Word file) and then activate Excel by simply clicking on the worksheet within your Word document.
   b. The Picture option pastes the worksheet contents as a picture that can be enlarged, reduced, or moved.

FORMULAS

WRITING FORMULAS

Formulas can be used to manipulate numeric data. They are entered just as they would be processed algebraically. For example, to add the values in cell C3 and cell C4, the following steps are necessary:

1. Choose any cell in which you want the result to appear and type: =C3+C4. When an equal sign is the very first thing entered, Excel knows it is a mathematical expression. If there is a space before the equal sign, Excel will read it as simply a group of characters.
2. Press "Enter" to place the results of the equation in the cell (i.e., 17 for this example; you may delete this entry once you are successful in obtaining the correct result).

The same process applies to subtraction, division, and multiplication. The multiplication symbol is the asterisk (*). The division symbol is the slash (/). Remember to use the equal sign as the beginning character so that the cell contents are identified as a formula.

COPYING FORMULAS

Now we will add the quantity supplied column to our robot worksheet. A survey reveals that there is a linear relationship between price and quantity supplied (QS) for our toy robots. QS is described by the mathematical equation: $QS = 0 + .1 * P$

We will use this formula in our worksheet to compute the quantity supplied. The heading "QS" should already be in cell E2. In the cell below QS, type the formula, substituting "P" with the cell location for price (A3). Thus, in cell E3 type: = 0 + .1*A3. Press enter and the number 1 should appear in the cell.

Instead of entering the formula into multiple cells, you can copy this formula into the other cells. The cell addresses will automatically adjust as you copy a formula from one cell to another. If a formula is copied down the length of a column, the address will change corresponding to the row in which the formula is placed. For example, in copying the formula from cell E3 to cell E4, the cell address for price will automatically change from A3 to A4. This is referred to as **relative addressing**. If a formula is copied across a row, the address will change corresponding to the changing columns. Copy the formula into the other cells in your worksheet by performing the following steps:

1. Click on the cell that contains the formula (E3). Put the cursor on the small box in the bottom right corner of the cell (the fill handle); the cursor will turn to a "+".
2. Drag the cell over the range of cells you want to fill (E4 through E12).

Your worksheet should now resemble Exhibit 2.5.

Exhibit 2.5 - Robot Worksheet				
Wacky Toy Robots by Robots-R-Us				
Price		QD		QS
10		9		1
20		8		2
30		7		3
40		6		4
50		5		5
60		4		6
70		3		7
80		2		8
90		1		9
100		0		10

The alternative to relative addressing is called **absolute addressing**. This means that the cell references do not adjust, but they remain exactly as they were in the source cell of the copy procedure. To make a formula absolute you must precede that portion of the formula with a dollar sign ($). Thus, if you want to copy a formula such as =C2*D5 and you want to make C2 an absolute address, you would type the formula as =C2*D5 before copying.

Special Features 3

This chapter presents information concerning special Excel features that are useful for economic analysis. The features include sorting, automatic sums, formulas, numeric formatting, and functions. In the newest version of Excel, a green triangle in the upper left corner of a cell indicates that a message accompanies that cell. Excel provides messages to inform you of a particular situation and the options available. Clicking on the cell will cause the message box to appear, and putting the cursor on the box will cause the actual message to appear. For example, if you used a formula to add some numbers within a column, but you did not include every number (either intentionally or unintentionally), then Excel would notify you that there are adjacent numbers that were not included in the formula. By clicking on the arrow within the message box, you are given the option to update the formula to include the adjacent cells.

✂ SPECIAL FEATURES ✄

First, create a new worksheet by clicking on the icon of a sheet of paper (the leftmost icon on the second toolbar). Assume that you are shopping around for the best prices on the college textbooks that you must purchase. Type the information from Exhibit 3.1 into the worksheet. Note that you will need to widen the columns in order to fit the words. You can first type in the word to determine how wide the column should be; remember to press enter in order to leave the edit mode. Review: To widen a column, position the cursor at the top of the screen on the mid-point between the lettered column headings (e.g. between A and B). After the cursor changes into a "+," drag the column to a different width.

Exhibit 3.1 - Textbook Costs Worksheet

	A	B	C
1	Textbook	Bookstore #1	Bookstore #2
2			
3	Microeconomics	90	100
4	World History	65	60
5	Speech	40	50
6	Auditing	95	90
7	Total Cost		
8			

SORTING WORDS AND NUMBERS

Excel will sort words or numbers in an ascending or descending manner. The "sort ascending" icon displays the letter A on top of the letter Z; it will sort a list going from A to Z. The "sort descending" icon displays the letter Z on top of the letter A.

Simply clicking on any cell within the column and then clicking on the sort icon can sort a column.

Using our worksheet, suppose the boss wants the textbooks listed in alphabetical order. For this example, multiple columns need to be sorted - the textbooks along with their corresponding costs. To sort multiple columns, highlight all the appropriate cells (i.e., cells A3 through C6). Once the cells are selected, click on the sort-ascending button. Excel will sort according to the data in the first column, either alphabetically or numerically. Your worksheet should look like the one shown in Exhibit 3.2.

Exhibit 3.2 - Textbook Costs Worksheet		
	A	**B**	**C**
1	Textbook	Bookstore #1	Bookstore #2
2			
3	Auditing	95	90
4	Microeconomics	90	100
5	Speech	40	50
6	World History	65	60
7	Total Cost		

The textbooks could be sorted by cost instead of alphabetically. To sort by cost, the menu bar must be used. First, highlight the range of cells to be sorted (i.e. cells A3 through C6). Click on Data in the menu bar and choose Sort. Select the column by which you want the list sorted, in this case we'll choose Bookstore #1 (column B). Excel gives the option to sort ascending or descending. Exhibit 3.3 lists the textbooks by ascending costs at Bookstore #1.

AUTOMATIC SUMS

Excel contains an icon with the Greek sigma sign (Σ). This icon is called Autosum and will automatically sum numbers within cells you select. Using the textbook worksheet, compute each column's total cost by using the following instructions:

1.　　Highlight the cells to be summed (for Bookstore #1: B3 through B6).
2.　　Click on the Autosum icon. The total will be inserted into the next cell.

In the newest version of Excel, the Autosum icon is accompanied by a down arrow. Upon clicking on the arrow, other functions will be displayed, such as averaging numbers and counting cells.

Note: If a number has more characters than a cell will hold, the number signs (####) will appear. To correct this, simply widen the column.

Repeat the Autosum process for Bookstore #2. The totals are shown in Exhibit 3.3. To enhance the appearance of the worksheet, place a line under the figures being summed (i.e., cells B6 and C6). To place an underscore in a cell, click on the appropriate cell and then click on the underscore icon (U).

Exhibit 3.3 - Textbook Costs Worksheet

	A	B	C
1	Textbook	Bookstore #1	Bookstore #2
2			
3	Speech	40	50
4	World History	65	60
5	Microeconomics	90	100
6	Auditing	95	90
7	Total Cost	290	300

FREEZE PANES

When working on a large worksheet, sometimes the entire worksheet does not fit on the screen. The Freeze Panes command allows you to freeze rows or columns. The cells on one side of the freeze line remain stationary, while the cells on the other side of the line can be scrolled. For example, a row of headings can be frozen while you scroll and view the remainder of the worksheet. Exhibit 3.4 illustrates freezing row 1; note that row 1 has remained at the top of the display, while the remaining worksheet has been scrolled to row 20. The Freeze Panes command allows you to compare any rows or columns of data that are not already adjacent on the worksheet.

Exhibit 3.4 - Freeze Panes

	A	B	C
1	A F F	B V F	T P P Y
2 0	4 0	0	0
2 1	4 0	6	1 0
2 2	4 0	1 1	2 0

To use the Freeze Panes option, perform the following steps:

1. Place the cell pointer where you want the freeze to be.
    a. For a **horizontal** freeze, the rows **above** the cell pointer will be frozen. Place the pointer in the first column of the appropriate row.
    b. For a **vertical** freeze, the columns to the **left** of the cell pointer will be frozen. Place the pointer in the top row of the appropriate column. (For Exhibit 3.4, the pointer was placed in cell A2.)
2. Click on "Window" in the menu bar and select the Freeze Panes option.

If the pointer is not placed in the first column or the first row, then horizontal and vertical splits will appear simultaneously. To remove the freeze, click on "Window" and select the Unfreeze Panes option.

IMPORTING DATA

Using the Clipboard feature, data from other spreadsheets or programs can be copied or "imported" into a Microsoft Excel worksheet.

1. Open the file that contains the data you want imported into your Excel worksheet. Select the data that you want copied and copy it to the Clipboard.
2. Select the area on the Excel worksheet to where the information should be imported and click on the Paste icon.

✧ NUMERIC FORMATTING ✧

Assume that you are asked to prepare a worksheet to calculate loan payments based on the information below. Type the data from Exhibit 3.5 into a new worksheet. Note that column A will need to be widened to accommodate the words "Annual Payment." Review: To widen a column, position the cursor on the mid-point between the lettered column headings. The cursor should change into a "+." Click-and-drag the column to a different width.

Exhibit 3.5 - Loan Payments Worksheet

	A	B	C	D
1	Rate	0.1	0.05	0.06
2	Years	10	20	8
3	Principal	100000	30000	20000
4	Annual Payment			

First, we will format the numbers in a simple manner using icons. Customized formatting using the menu bar will also be discussed. After formatting, we will calculate the annual payment using an Excel function.

PERCENTAGE SYMBOL

Select the cells that need percentages and click on the icon that displays the percentage symbol (%). For our example, select the cells B1 through D1 that contain the rate. As shown in Exhibit 3.6, the numbers are converted to percentages.

CURRENCY STYLE

The icon of a dollar sign ($) is called "currency style" and will automatically add dollar sign, decimal, and cents places to any cell you select. In your worksheet, select the cells that contain values for Principal and click on the dollar icon. The columns will automatically widen to accommodate the numerical formatting.

If you accidentally insert a currency style into the wrong cell, you must go to the Format menu to un-format the cell. Click on the Format menu and choose Cells. Under the Number tab choose Currency. Excel will offer several options; scroll untill you select "None" for symbols and "2" for the number of decimal places. Variations in currency formats are described in the Customized Formatting section.

COMMAS

To insert commas into the principal payments in the worksheet, select cells B3 through D3. Click on the icon that displays a comma. You will note that the columns automatically widened to accommodate the numerical formatting. Your worksheet should now resemble Exhibit 3.6.

Exhibit 3.6 - Loan Payments Worksheet			
Rate	10%	5%	6%
Years	10	20	8
Principal	$100,000.00	$30,000.00	$20,000.00
Annual Payment			

CUSTOMIZED FORMATTING

If you need a format other than what the icons provide, you can customize the formatting of a cell through the menu bar. For percentages, any number of decimal places may be used. For numbers and currency, you are given the option of using parentheses, a negative sign, a dollar sign, and the number of decimal places. To customize a cell:

1. Highlight the cells to be formatted.
2. Click on Format in the menu bar and select Cells.
3. Choose the category and options you desire.

Exhibit 3.7 displays some of the variations in numeric formatting.

Exhibit 3.7 - Examples of Available Numeric Formats	
Format Type	**Display**
Number	1234 1,234.00 (any number of decimal places may be chosen) -1,234.56 (negative number can also be in parenthesis or in red)
Date	3/14 3/14/98 March - 98 March 14, 1998 3/14/98 1:30 PM Some options have the time displayed along with the date.
Time	13:30 1:30 PM 13:30:55
Percentage	5% or 5.00% (any number of decimal places may be chosen)
Currency	$1,234 $1,234.00 (any number of decimal places may be chosen) $(1,234.56) negative number
Special	Numbers can be formatted as zip codes, phone numbers, or Social Security numbers.

✑ FUNCTIONS ✑

Functions are basically pre-written formulas. They save time and increase accuracy. To calculate the annual payments for our example loan payments worksheet, the use of the @PMT function will be explained below.

1. Click on the cell in which you want the annual payment to appear (B4).
2. Click on the "fx" icon that represents the Functions Wizard.
3. Choose Financial under the Functions category box.

4.   Choose PMT under the Function name box. Then click OK.
5.   Enter the cell locations that contain the rate, nper, and pv. Use the mouse to click on the different boxes. In this example, the rate is B1. Nper (years) is B2. Pv (principal) is B3. (The formula is =PMT(rate, nper, pv). Excel will also ask for fv and type; leave those blank. Click on OK.

Excel should have automatically calculated "($16,274.54)" in the cell. Do not use the Functions Wizard to calculate the remaining annual payments; instead we will save time by copying the formula into the other cells. Review: To copy a formula, click on the cell that contains the formula (B4). Put the cursor on the small box in the bottom right corner of the cell; the cursor will turn into a "+". Drag the cell over the range of cells you want to fill (C4 and D4).

Exhibit 3.8 includes the annual loan payment calculations.

Exhibit 3.8 - Loan Payments Worksheet			
Rate	10%	5%	6%
Years	10	20	8
Principal	$100,000.00	$30,000.00	$20,000.00
Annual Payment	($16,274.54)	($2,407.28)	($3,220.72)

The Functions Wizard of Excel has many useful functions available in addition to those that perform basic arithmetic. Some functions and their symbols are described in Exhibit 3.9.

Exhibit 3.9 - Excel Functions

Financial Functions:

FV	Returns the future value of an investment.
IPMT	Returns the interest payment for an investment for a given period.
IRR	Returns the internal rate of return for a series of cash flows.
NPV	Returns the net present value of an investment based on a series of periodic cash flows and a discount rate.
PMT	Returns period payments for an annuity.
PV	Returns the present value of an investment.
RATE	Returns the interest rate per period of an annuity.

Date and Time Functions:

DATE	Returns the serial number of a particular date.
DAY	Converts a serial number to a particular day of the month.
DAYS360	Calculates the number of days between two dates based on a 360-day year.
TIMEVALUE	Converts the time in the form of text to a serial number.
TODAY	Returns the serial number of today's date.

Math and Trig Functions:

COUNTIF	Returns the number of nonblank cells in a given range which meet the given criteria.
INT	Rounds a number down to the nearest integer.
ROUND	Rounds a number to the specified number of digits.
SUBTOTAL	Returns a subtotal in a list or database.
SUM	Adds the specified numbers.

Statistical Functions:

AVERAGE	Returns the average of the specified numbers.
COUNT	Counts how many numbers are in a given range.
MAX	Returns the maximum number in a specified range.
MEDIAN	Returns the median of the specified numbers.
MIN	Returns the minimum number in a specified range.
MODE	Returns the most common value in a specified range.

Charts and Worksheet Manipulation 4

The spreadsheet program allows you to create charts or graphs as a way to visually represent numeric data. Excel refers to both charts and graphs as simply "charts." Before creating any chart, the data that is to be used in the chart must first be typed into a worksheet. Next, highlight the data and click on the Chart Wizard icon (picture of blue, yellow, and red columns on a bar chart). The Chart Wizard will guide you through a four-step process of creating a chart. A chart is linked to the worksheet data from which it is created and automatically revises itself when the data in the worksheet is changed. The following sections provide specific directions on creating the most commonly used chart for economics, a line chart.

📑 LINE CHART 📑

A line chart is used for plotting data on a vertical y-axis and a horizontal x-axis. The y-axis can contain from one to six ranges, producing one to six lines. In preparation for creating a chart, construct a new worksheet containing the data in Exhibit 4.1. Using this data, we will create two line charts: the first showing total revenue (TR), and the second showing price (P), marginal revenue (MR), and the price elasticity coefficient of demand (PEC(D)).

MAKING THE TOTAL REVENUE CHART

In creating a chart, you must **first** paint in the range on the worksheet containing the data that is to be charted; in this case that would be the column containing the total revenue values and the heading "TR" (cells E2 to E6). Next, click on the Chart Wizard icon (a colorful bar chart). There are four steps in Chart Wizard.

	Exhibit 4.1 - Revenue Worksheet				
	A	**B**	**C**	**D**	**E**
1	Output Area:				
2	Q	P	MR	PEC(D)	TR
3	0	30			0
4	40	22	16	-2.75	880
5	80	14	0	-0.88	1120
6	120	6	-16	-0.25	720

STEP ONE

In the first step, you must select a type of chart. Select Line chart. Then you may choose any of the variations of line charts offered. When completed, click on "Next."

STEP TWO

In step two, Chart Wizard is confirming the data range, which you previously highlighted, and the fact that your data is in columns. Also, you can designate the values for the x-axis in this step. Click on the "Series" tab and then click on the box showing "Category (X) axis labels." On your worksheet, highlight the range showing quantity values, not the title (cells A3 to A6). Press return. The result appears in Exhibit 4.2. Chart Wizard will immediately enter the quantity amounts for the x-axis. Click on "Next."

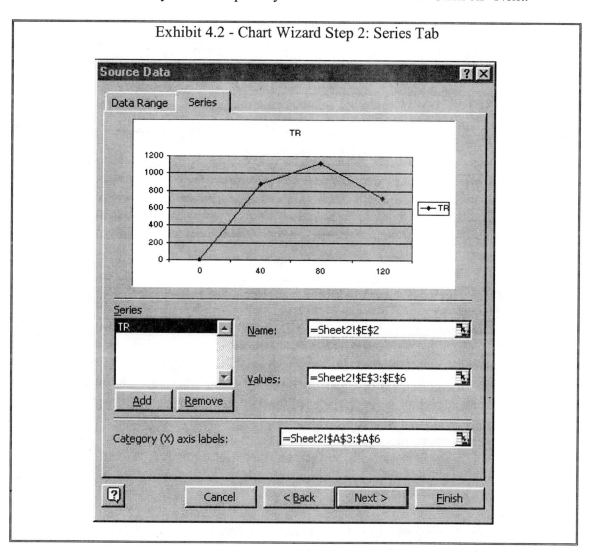

Exhibit 4.2 - Chart Wizard Step 2: Series Tab

STEP THREE

In step three, chart options may be selected, such as titles, legend, data labels, and gridlines. Type "Total Revenue" into the title box. Type "Quantity" into the x-axis box and "Dollars" into the y-axis box. Chart Wizard automatically uses gridlines corresponding to the y-axis. To include gridlines for the x-axis, click on the "gridlines" tab and check the box corresponding to x-axis gridlines.

Chart Wizard will automatically show a chart legend unless you turn the option off. If the column headings had not been highlighted initially, then Chart Wizard would use the generic label of "Series 1" for the legend. Values or symbols can be placed directly on the lines charted by clicking on the Data Labels tab.

STEP FOUR

In step four, you will indicate whether to save the chart as a new sheet or within your current worksheet. Select the latter. Click "Finish" and your chart will appear on your worksheet. Exhibit 4.3 contains the total revenue chart.

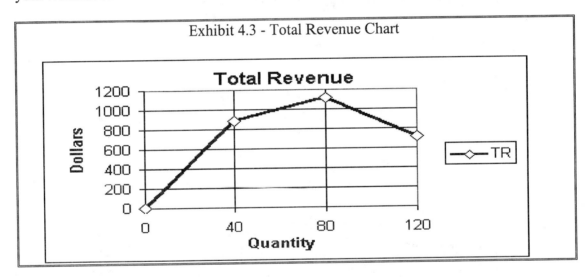

Exhibit 4.3 - Total Revenue Chart

To print a chart, highlight it and select "Print" or "Print-preview." Print-preview allows you to first make setup changes such as size and page orientation (portrait or landscape). To delete a chart, simply click on the chart and press the Delete key.

A chart can be modified **after** completing Chart Wizard. Simply left-click on a specific part of the chart and choose to re-format. To modify any of the chart options from step 3 (title, gridlines, legend, etc), right-click on the chart (between gridlines) to access "chart options." The following changes were made to the chart in Exhibit 4.3.

Chart Options:
- ✓ Background: The background area was changed to white by right-clicking on the chart area and accessing the Format Plot Area menu box. Several colors and border styles are available.

✓   Line: To modify the style of the "total revenue" line, we accessed the Format Data Series by right clicking on the total revenue line and selecting a different style and background color.

✓   Chart Size and Position: The chart can be enlarged or reduced by clicking and moving its borders like any other box. The chart can be repositioned on the worksheet by clicking on it and dragging it to a new position.

✓   X-axis: Excel automatically positions the category labels (Quantity) between the tick marks on the x-axis and thus plots the values between the tick marks. You can change this and create a direct alignment by right-clicking on the category axis (x-axis) and bringing up the Format Axis menu box, as shown in Exhibit 4.4. Next, click on the "Scale" tab and un-check the first small box next to "Value (Y) axis crosses between categories."

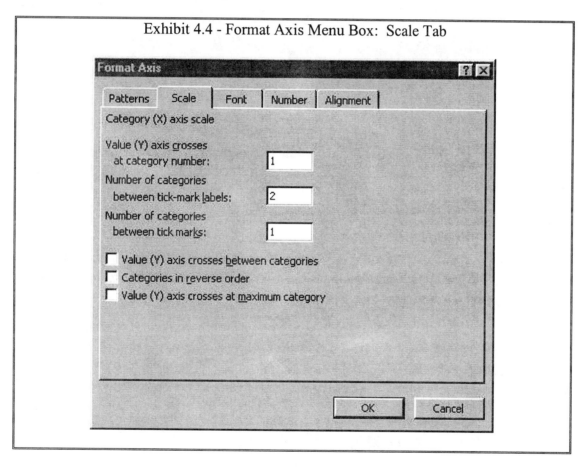

Exhibit 4.4 - Format Axis Menu Box: Scale Tab

✓   Axis numbers: By clicking on the Alignment tab (shown in Exhibit 4.5), you can position the numbers along the axis at 90 degrees or any angle; this makes the large numbers easier to read.

Exhibit 4.5 - Format Axis Menu Box: Alignment Tab

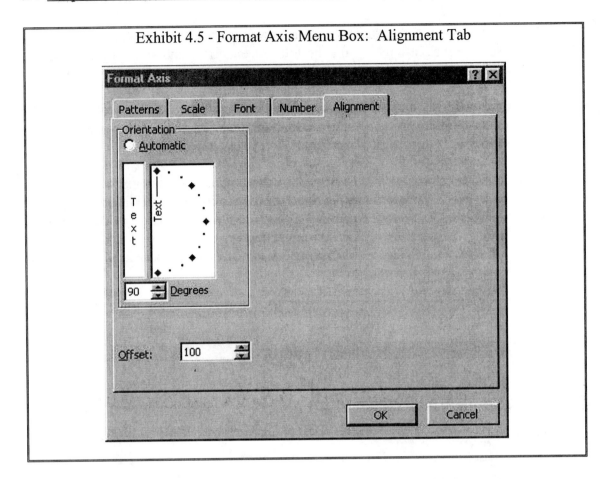

MAKING THE P, MR, AND PEC(D) CHART

To make this chart, first highlight the range containing the P, MR, and PEC(D) data (cells B2 through D6), which includes the column headings. Next, click on the Chart Wizard icon and go through the four steps described above. Remember to insert the range for quantity in Step 2. The resulting chart appears in Exhibit 4.6.

You will note that the values for the x-axis were reformatted so that the numbers are located at the bottom of the chart instead of next to the axis in the middle of the chart. This can be accomplished by right-clicking on the x-axis to bring up the "Format axis" menu box. Next, click on the "Patterns" tab and change the "Tick mark labels" from "next to axis" to "low."

OTHER TYPES OF CHARTS

Chart Wizard offers 15 other types of charts, such as bar, column, pie, and donut. The four-step process is the same for each type of chart. You should use the type of chart that best conveys the meaning of the data you are presenting. In the case of demand and supply, we want to convey the linear relationship of the demand and supply curves, and to draw attention to the equilibrium point where the curves intersect.

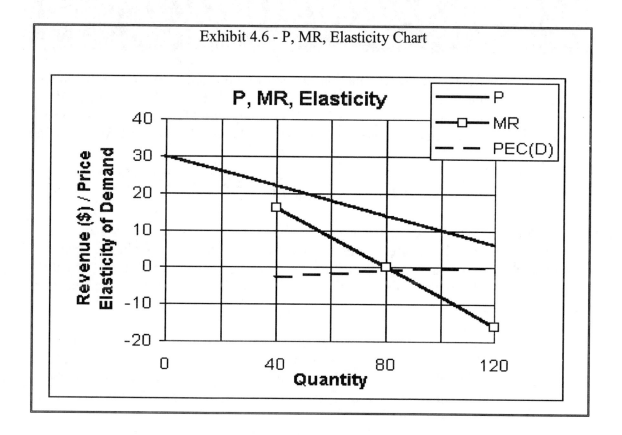

Exhibit 4.6 - P, MR, Elasticity Chart

Data Manipulation 5

Excel provides a database function that allows you to assimilate and manipulate related information. A database is comprised of records that are comprised of fields. A field is a single item of data such as price (P), total revenue (TR), or marginal revenue (MR). A record is a group of related fields such as the P, TR, and MR for a specific quantity.

AUTOFILL

This command enables the user to fill a specified range with a sequence of numbers or text (e.g. 1st quarter). The numbers can be consecutive or in increments of any size. We will use the Autofill function on a new worksheet. First, type "Quantity" into cell A1. We'll create a column with numbers ranging from 0 to 40 in increments of 10 by using the following steps:

1. Type in the first two values of the series (i.e., 0 and 10) in the first two cells below the heading (A2 and A3).
2. Highlight the cells in which you just placed your values. Put the cursor on the small box in the bottom right corner of the cell (the fill handle); the cursor will turn to a "+".
3. Click and drag your mouse over the cells that you want AutoFill to fill. In this case, that would be cells A4 to A6. Release the mouse.

In the latest version of Excel, a message box accompanies the Autofill command. The box offers the options of filling in the cells with or without formatting, and also gives the option to copy the cells instead of filling.

DATA FORM

You will now add data to the worksheet created above, but instead of typing the data into each cell, you will use an Excel feature called data form. The purpose of data form is to reduce errors resulting from entering data into the wrong cell. When using data form, you provide Excel with the titles you want on the worksheet and it inserts these titles into a simplified form. You can then add information record by record.

You have already entered quantity (Q) into your worksheet, but there is not an empty row in which to place a heading. To insert a row, click on cell A1, select the Insert menu and choose Row. Type "Q" into cell A1. Now insert the remaining data from

Exhibit 5.1 into your worksheet by performing the following steps. (Note: for this example, we will not take the time to enter data for all of the quantities just created.)

1. Type the titles (AR, TR, MR) onto the first row of the worksheet and highlight them.
2. Select Data on the menu bar and choose the Form option. If you are asked whether the 1st row should be used as label; click "OK."
3. The form will automatically appear with your titles as the field names on the form. You can now begin entering data from your records. IMPORTANT: Use the Tab key when moving from one field to the next. Hit the Enter key at the end of each record.

Exhibit 5.1 - Example Data

Q	AR	TR	MR
0	155	0	155
10	145	1450	135
20	135	2700	115
30	125	3750	95
40	115	4600	75

When finished, the worksheet should resemble Exhibit 5.2.

Exhibit 5.2 - Results of Data Form

	A	B	C	D
1	Q	A R	T R	M R
2	0	155	0	155
3	10	145	1450	135
4	20	135	2700	115
5	30	125	3750	95
6	40	115	4600	75

☙ DATA SORT ☙

While designing a worksheet, you may decide to rearrange data within a column. Suppose you want "Quantity" to start with 40 and descend to zero. To perform this sort, execute the following steps:

1. Select the database information that you want to sort. You'll be highlighting each record in its entirety since we want each record to remain intact as it is sorted. Highlight the data below the titles, cells A2

through D6. (It is not a problem if you highlight the titles because Excel will ask if you have a title row.)

2.   Select "Data" in the menu bar and choose the Sort option.

3.   In the Sort box, select which field to sort by (the first column is automatically selected) and whether to sort in ascending or descending order. Note that you can choose to have three "tiers" of fields by which to sort.

☠ AUTOFILTER ☠

This command permits the user to select and view records in a database that meet a specific criteria set forth by the user. You determine your criteria by selecting what data from which fields you want to keep. For example, you may choose to see only those records that have marginal revenue of 115 or more. AutoFilter will allow you to do this by performing the following steps:

1.   Highlight all of the records including the titles.

2.   Click on "Data" in the menu bar. Choose the Filter option and then the AutoFilter.

3.   Small boxes with down arrows will appear in each cell containing a field title. These drop boxes will list options when the arrow is clicked.

4.   In order to view only those records that have marginal revenue of 115 or more, click on the down arrow in the MR cell. Several options will appear; choose the Custom option. (If you selected one of the numbers displayed, then only those records containing that number would be shown.)

5.   In the Custom AutoFilter menu box, click on the arrow within the first box in order to view your options. Select the "is greater than or equal to" option. Then, click on the next box to the right and type in "115." Click the OK button.

Your worksheet should now display only those records that have a MR of 115 or more, as shown in Exhibit 5.3. To delete the AutoFilter, once again click on Data, then Filter, and uncheck the AutoFilter option by clicking on it.

	A	B	C	D
			Exhibit 5.3 - Results of AutoFilter		
1	Q	AR	TR	MR
2	0	155	0	155
3	10	145	1450	135
4	20	135	2700	115

Guidelines for Worksheet Design 6

This chapter discusses the general guidelines that should be considered when designing a worksheet: (1) Create a file identification area; (2) Construct an input area; (3) Construct an output area; (4) Enter data in rows or columns, but not both; (5) Create backup files; and (6) Test the worksheet.

⚑ FILE IDENTIFICATION AREA ⚑

A file identification area (i.e. worksheet heading information) should be prepared at the top of the worksheet. This area should include pertinent information such as:
- file name
- worksheet designer's name
- input required (what input is necessary to solve the problem at hand?)
- output that will be generated
- the dates the file was created, modified, and last used

These details should be determined before beginning work. For example, assume you are required to create a worksheet that shows the breakeven point in units and dollars for your firm's product. Exhibit 6.1 shows the file identification area for such a worksheet.

Exhibit 6.1 - File Identification Area

	A	B	C	D	E	F
1	FILE IDENTIFICATION AREA					
2	Filename: Product X Breakeven Analysis					
3	Designer: Mike Duke					
4	Input Required:					
5		a. market price for a good: P				
6		b.average variable cost: AVC				
7		c. total fixed cost: FC				
8	Output: Breakeven Analysis					
9		a. breakeven point in units (Q_{BE})				
10		b. breakeven point in dollars (TR_{BE})				
11	File Created: 5/21/xx					
12	File Modified: 5/31/xx					
13	File Last Used: 7/15/xx					
14						

INPUT AREA

The input area of a worksheet contains the data items necessary for using the worksheet. In this case, the input area contains the values for the market price for the good (P), average variable cost (AVC), and total fixed cost (FC). These values are manually entered into one column of the input area. Exhibit 6.2 shows the input area for our breakeven analysis example.

OUTPUT AREA

The output area contains the desired outcome; in this case, the breakeven point in units and dollars for your firm's product. Exhibit 6.2 contains the example output area.

Instead of manually inserting values within the output area, formulas are inserted. Values for the output area are then computed based on amounts within the input area. For our example worksheet, the titles (i.e., P, AVC, contribution margin, etc.) and their corresponding formulas were entered into the output area. The output area is then formula driven. This enables the user to change any value displayed in the input area and instantly know what the corresponding breakeven point is. The formulas used in the worksheet are shown at the bottom of Exhibit 6.2.

INPUT ALIGNMENT

For maximum efficiency, the input cells should be aligned vertically (in a column) or horizontally (in a row), but not both. Fewer mistakes should occur if the user doesn't have to steer the cursor through a maze of input cells.

MANUAL RECALCULATION

When working with large worksheets, it is helpful to turn off Excel's automatic recalculation if more than one value in the input area is to be changed. This is due to the fact that the software instantly recalculates mathematical expressions once a value has been modified. Data cannot be entered while the recalculations are taking place. The time involved is inconsequential for small worksheets but can become a burden for large worksheets. A simple procedure is used to change from automatic recalculation to manual recalculation. Select the Tools menu and choose Options. Select the Calculation sheet. In the Calculation area, choose Manual. After choosing this command, the F9 key must be pressed for recalculation to occur.

TESTING

Any new worksheet should be manually tested. If formulas are involved, the user must test the worksheet result against an example that is already proven correct.

	A	B	C	D	E	F
1	**FILE IDENTIFICATION AREA**					
2	Filename: Product X Breakeven Analysis					
3	Designer: Mike Duke					
4	Input Required:					
5		a. market price for a good: P				
6		b.average variable cost: AVC				
7		c. total fixed cost: FC				
8	Output: Breakeven Analysis					
9		a. breakeven point in units (Q_{BE})				
10		b. breakeven point in dollars (TR_{BE})				
11	File Created: 5/21/xx					
12	File Modified: 5/31/xx					
13	File Last Used: 7/15/xx					
14						
15	**INPUT AREA:**					
16		P:			$12	
17		AVC:			$8	
18		FC:			$10,000	
19						
20	**OUTPUT AREA:**					
21		P:			$12.00	
22		AVC:			$8.00	
23						
24		Contribution Margin:			$4.00	
25						
26		Fixed Cost:			$10,000	
27						
28		Breakeven point in units (Q_{BE}):			2500	
29		(quantity at breakeven)				
30		Breakeven Point in dollars (TR_{BE}):			$30,000	
31		(total revenue at breakeven)				
32	Formulas (relationships) used in output area:					
33	Sales Price (P):			Given constant value		=E16
34	Variable cost (AVC):			Given constant value		=E17
35	Contribution margin:			=P-AVC		=E16-E17
36	Fixed cost (FC):			Given constant value		=E18
37	Breakeven point in units (Q_{BE}):			=FC/(P-AVC)		=E18/E24
38	Breakeven point in dollars (TR_{BE}			=Q_{BE}*P		=E28*E16
39				=(FC/(P-AVC))*P		

Exhibit 6.2 - Breakeven Analysis Worksheet

Step-by-Step   7
Excel Example

This chapter provides step-by-step instructions for creating a simple worksheet and chart using Microsoft Excel spreadsheet software.

☺   CREATING AN EXCEL WORKSHEET   ☺

Open a new worksheet. The letters across the top of a worksheet correspond to columns. The numbers along the left side of a worksheet correspond to rows. The box at the intersection of a column and row is referred to as the cell location. Text or mathematical expressions are entered into a cell by clicking on the cell and typing. Press "Enter" to enter the data into the worksheet.

☺   FILE IDENTIFICATION AND INPUT AREA   ☺

In constructing a worksheet, the first step is to provide file identification and the input information that will be needed for the desired output. The objective of this worksheet will be to illustrate supply and demand. Click on the appropriate cell and enter the initial information shown in Exhibit 7.1. Use Autofill to insert the values for quantity. Brief reviews of some of the Excel features are given if you should need them.

In order to prepare a chart of the supply and demand curves, the relationships must be written in terms of price being a function of quantity. P(Qd) is the market demand relationship expressed as price being a function of quantity. P(Qs) is the market supply relationship expressed as price being a function of quantity.

AUTOFILL

This command enables the user to fill a specified range with a sequence of numbers.

1. Type in the first two values of the series (i.e., 0 and 10) in the first two cells below the heading (B17 and B18).
2. Highlight the cells in which you just placed your values. Put the cursor on the small box in the bottom right corner of the cell (the fill handle); the cursor will turn to a "+".
3. Click and drag your mouse over the cells that you want Autofill to fill in. Release the mouse.

	A	B	C	D	E	F	G
	Exhibit 7.1 - File Id and Input Area for Example Worksheet						
1	FILE IDENTIFICATION AREA						
2	Filename: DemandSupply.xls						
3	Designer:						
4	Input Required:						
5		a. quantity: Q					
6		b. demand relationship expressed as price being a function of quantity: P(Qd)					
7		c. supply relationship expressed as price being a function of quantity: P(Qs)					
8	Output: Supply and Demand Schedules						
9		a. quantity demanded at market prices (Qd)					
10		b. quantity supplied at market prices (Qs)					
11	File Created:						
12	File Modified:						
13	File Last Used:						
14							
15	INPUT AREA:						
16		**Q** (Qd or Qs)	**P(Qd)**	**P(Qs)**			
17		0	=40-.2*Qd	=5+.5*Qs			
18		10					
19		20					
20		30					
21		40					
22		50					
23		60					
24		70					
25		80					
26		90					
27		100					
28							

EDITING A CELL

A cell can be put into edit mode by double clicking on the cell. Excel will then allow you to move around within the cell and change the contents. A cell can also be edited within the formula bar at the top of the worksheet. When a cell is clicked on, its contents automatically appear in the formula bar. The cell's contents may be centered, underlined, the font changed, or anything else that can be done to regular text. When finished typing, press "Enter" to insert the contents into the worksheet. To delete the entire contents of a cell, click on the cell and press the Delete or Backspace key.

INSERTING FORMULAS

Formulas are entered just as they would be processed algebraically, using cell addresses to represent values in the equation. When an equal sign is the very first symbol entered, Excel knows this cell contains a mathematical expression. If there is a space before the equal sign, Excel will read it as text only. Do not put any spaces within the formula. Type the formulas from Exhibit 7.1 into your worksheet; press "Enter" after each cell entry.

COLUMN EXPANSION

When the spreadsheet program is first loaded, the column width will be eight characters. If your cell data exceeds the cell width, the data will simply run into the adjacent empty cell. However, if the adjacent cell is not empty, the overflow data will be truncated at the cell border. To avoid this, column width can be changed using the following steps. Note: It is best to be out of the edit mode when changing cell width; click on a blank cell to exit the edit mode.
1.   Position the cursor at the top of the screen on the mid-point between the lettered column headings (i.e., between A and B). The cursor should change into a "+."
2.   Click-and-drag using the left mouse key; hold it while "dragging" the column to a different width.

☺   OUTPUT AREA   ☺

Using the demand relationship: =40-2*Qd, we will compute the data for the quantity demanded at each of the price data points (P). Likewise, using the supply relationship: =5+.5*Qs, we will compute the data for the quantity supplied.

Format the output area by typing in the formulas from Exhibit 7.2. Note that the formulas now contain the appropriate cell addresses. The values for quantity (Q) can be taken directly from the input area. Copy the formulas into the remaining cells for Q, P(Qd), and P(Qs) using the Autofill procedure as discussed below.

COPYING FORMULAS

Cell addresses will automatically adjust when a formula is copied from one cell to another. If a formula is copied down the length of a column using the Autofill procedure, the address will change corresponding to the row in which the formula is placed. This is referred to as relative addressing. If a formula is copied across a row, the address will change corresponding to the changing columns. Copy the formula into the other cells in your worksheet by performing the following steps:
1.   Click on the cell that contains the formula. Put the cursor on the small box in the bottom right corner of the cell (the fill handle); the cursor will turn to a "+".

2.	Drag the cell over the range of cells you want to fill.

Exhibit 7.2 - Output Format for Example Worksheet

28				
29	Output Area:			
30		Q	P(Qd)	P(Qs)
31		=B17	=40-(0.2*B17)	=5+(0.5*B17)
32				

Note: These cells show the typed formula before pressing "Enter."

After inserting and copying the formulas, the output area of the worksheet should now contain the correct values for each item, as shown in Exhibit 7.3. Note that the cells show the result of the calculations made within each cell based on its formula. The procedure for inserting dollar signs is explained in the following section on Numeric Formatting.

Exhibit 7.3 - Output Area of Example Worksheet

	A	B	C	D
29	OUTPUT AREA:			
30		Q	P(Qd)	P(Qs)
31		0	$40	$5
32		10	$38	$10
33		20	$36	$15
34		30	$34	$20
35		40	$32	$25
36		50	$30	$30
37		60	$28	$35
38		70	$26	$40
39		80	$24	$45
40		90	$22	$50
41		100	$20	$55

MANIPULATING DATA

The worksheet just created can be used for any quantity amounts by simply changing the values in the input area. The user can modify the input area and instantly see how the change affects the output. The demand and supply formulas in the output area can be changed also. For example, change the value of the last quantity amount in the input area from 100 to 300. You'll note that the corresponding P(Qd) and P(Qs) values in the output were automatically recalculated.

NUMERIC FORMATTING

If you wish to include dollar signs and commas, highlight the cells containing currency values. Once the cells are selected, click on the icon of a dollar sign ($). Alternatively, you can click on "Format" in the menu bar and then select Cells - Number - Currency. To insert decimal places, click on Format - Cells - Number - Decimal places.

☺ CREATING A LINE CHART ☺

Having constructed a worksheet of the demand and supply data, we can now create a line chart from it. In creating a chart, you must **first** paint in the range on the worksheet containing the data that is to be charted, in this case that would be the columns containing P(Qd) and P(Qs) values and titles (cells C30 through D41). Next, click on the Chart Wizard icon (a colorful bar chart). There are four steps in Chart Wizard.

STEP ONE

In the first step, you must select a type of chart. Select "Line chart." Then you may choose any of the variations of line charts offered. When completed, click on "Next."

STEP TWO

In step two, Chart Wizard is confirming the data range, which you previously highlighted, and the fact that the data is in columns. Also, you can designate the values for the x-axis in this step. Click on the "Series" tab and then click on the box showing "Category (X) axis labels." On your worksheet, highlight the range showing quantity values, not the title (cells B31 to B41). Press "Enter." Chart Wizard will immediately enter the quantity amounts for the x-axis labels. Click on "Next."

STEP THREE

In step three, chart options may be selected, such as titles, gridlines, legend, and data labels. Type "Demand and Supply" into the title box. Type "Quantity" into the x-axis box and "Prices" into the y-axis box.

Chart Wizard automatically inserts gridlines corresponding to the y-axis. To include gridlines corresponding to the x-axis, click on the gridlines tab and check the box for x-axis gridlines. These are the only selections necessary for this example. Chart Wizard will automatically show a chart legend unless you turn the option off. If the column headings had not been highlighted initially, then Chart Wizard would use the generic label of "Series 1" for the legend.

Values or symbols can be placed directly on the graph lines by clicking on the Data Labels tab.

STEP FOUR

In step four, you will indicate whether to save the chart as a new sheet or within your current worksheet. Select the latter. Click "Finish" and your chart will appear on your worksheet. Exhibit 7.4 contains the demand and supply chart.

To print a chart, highlight it and select "Print" or "Print-preview." Print-preview allows you to first make setup changes such as size and page orientation (portrait or landscape). To delete a chart from your worksheet, simply click on the chart and press the Delete key.

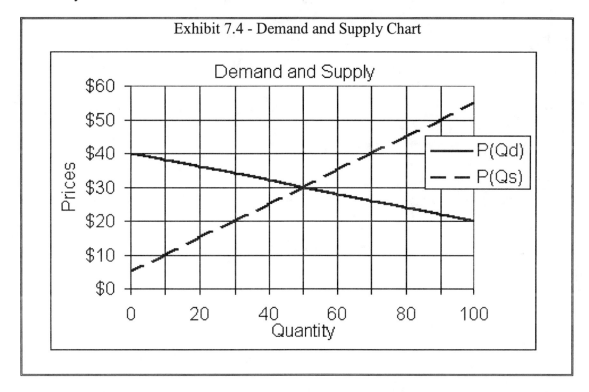

Exhibit 7.4 - Demand and Supply Chart

A chart can be modified **after** completing Chart Wizard. Simply right-click on a specific part of the chart and choose to re-format. For example, the following changes were made to the chart in Exhibit 7.4.

Chart Options:
✓ Background: The background area was changed to white by right-clicking on the chart area and accessing the Format Plot Area menu box. Several colors and border styles are made available.

✓ Line: To modify the style of the P(Qs) line, we accessed the Format Data Series by right-clicking on the P(Qs) line and selecting a different style and background color.

✓   Chart Size and Position: The chart can be enlarged or reduced by clicking and moving its borders like any other box. The chart can be repositioned on the worksheet by clicking on it and dragging it to a new position.

✓   X-axis: Excel automatically positions the category labels (Quantity) between the tick marks on the x-axis and thus plots the values between the tick marks. You can change this and create a direct alignment with the x-axis values by right-clicking on the category axis (x-axis) and bringing up the Format Axis menu box (shown on p. 22). Next, click on the "Scale" tab and un-check the first small box next to "Value (Y) axis crosses between categories."

Worksheet Assignments

LIST OF WORKSHEET ASSIGNMENTS (Page 1 of 2)

Introduction to Economics	Perfect Competition
1. Real versus nominal prices*	26. Unit cost and revenue analysis*
2. Calculating real wage	27. Unit cost and revenue analysis
	28. Unit cost and revenue analysis
Supply and Demand	29. Unit cost and revenue analysis
3. Supply and demand*	30. Profit analysis*
4. Change in demand*	31. Profit analysis
5. Change in demand	32. Profit analysis
6. Change in supply	33. Profit analysis
7. Change in both demand and supply	34. Profit analysis
	35. Short run supply for the perfect
Elasticity	competitor*
8. Price elasticity of demand*	
9. Price elasticity of demand	**Market Efficiency**
10. Income elasticity of demand	36. Consumer and producer surplus
11. Income elasticity of demand	
12. Cross price elasticity of demand	**Public Goods and Taxes**
13. Cross price elasticity of demand	37. Impact of a tax
14. Price elasticity of supply	38.Impact of price elasticity on tax burden
15. Price elasticity of supply	39.Impact of price elasticity on tax burden
Consumer Choice	**Government Intervention**
16. Indifference curves*	40. Effect of minimum wage on the
17. Budget constraint	market for labor
18. Price change effect on budget constraint	41. Impact of a price ceiling
19. Utility analysis*	**Efficiency, Monopoly, and**
20. Utility analysis - deriving demand	**Monopolistic Competition**
	42. Economies of scale
Production and Cost	43. Monopolist unit revenue
21. Production function*	44. Monopolist profit*
22. Total and marginal product*	45. Impact of subsidy on profit
23. Production analysis	46. Monopolistic competition
24. Total cost analysis	long run equilibrium
25. Unit cost analysis	

* The solution to this assignment is included at the end of the book.

LIST OF WORKSHEET ASSIGNMENTS (Page 2 of 2)

The Labor Market	Scarcity, Public Choice, and
47. Perfect competitor's marginal revenue product	**Public Policy**
	54. Production possibilities frontier curve*
48. Monopolist's marginal revenue product	55. Effect of technology on output using production possibilities frontier analysis
49. Labor demand and supply	56. Marginal analysis
50. Monopsony	57. Negative externality
	58. Positive externality
Investment Decision	
51. Present value*	**International Trade**
52. Future value	59. Impact of an import quota*
53. Investment decision	60. Impact of an import quota
	61. Impact of a tariff
	62. Impact of a tariff
	63. Foreign exchange rate
	64. Foreign exchange rate
	65. Comparative advantage*
	66. International comparative advantage

* The solution to this assignment is included at the end of the book.

1. REAL VERSUS NOMINAL PRICES*

Create a worksheet using the following information that shows the average market price of milk and the Consumer Price Index (CPI) from 1980 to 1998 at selected intervals, using two different base years for the CPI.

INPUT AREA:					
	1980	1985	1990	1995	1998
Market price	$1.05	$1.13	$1.39	$1.48	$1.61
CPI (1980)	100	130.58	158.62	184.95	197.82
CPI (1990)	63.04	82.34	100	116.60	124.71
OUTPUT AREA:					
Real price (1980 $)					
Real price (1990 $)					

Calculate the real price of milk in 1980 dollars and in 1990 dollars by inserting the appropriate formula into the worksheet.
Market/real price relationship: real P=(P/CPI)*100

2. CALCULATING REAL WAGE

Wages are the price of labor services. Since they are a market price for particular types of labor, they are subject to the effects of inflation as are all market prices. The wage or salary received by members of households is the largest single source of income in this country. Most people are interested in how their standard of living is progressing. Is it always true that if wage or salary increases, a person is materially better off (more goods and services can be purchased)?

a.   Using the information provided below, construct a worksheet to calculate real wage. Using the market/real wage relationship, calculate the real wage for each profession listed for the years shown.
Input Area:

Year	1990	1995	1998
Wage 1 (computer programmer)	$24,000	$31,000	$42,000
Wage 2 (teacher)	$17,000	$19,850	$21,300
Wage 3 (sales representative)	$13,000	$14,000	$14,500
CPI (1990)	100	116.60	124.71

Market/real wage relationship: real W=(W/CPI)*100

b. Create a line chart showing how each profession's real wage changed over this entire time period. Use years as the x-axis data.

c. What does it mean in terms of material standard of living when real wage increases?

d. What does it mean in terms of material standard of living when real wage remains constant?

e. What does it mean in terms of material standard of living when real wage decreases?

f. What could have happened to the number of college students interested in studying computer programming over this period of time based on real wages?

3. **SUPPLY AND DEMAND***

a. Prepare a worksheet with a column of price from $0 to $50 in $5 increments. Using the demand relationship: Qd = 110 - 2*P, compute the data for the quantity demanded at each of the price data points. Do likewise for quantity supplied using the supply relationship: Qs = -10 + 2*P. At what price and quantity will the market be in equilibrium?

b. In order to prepare a chart of the supply and demand curves from this data, you must express each of these relationships in terms of price being a function of quantity. In this case, the equivalent relationships are:

P(Qd) = 55 - .5*Qd
P(Qs) = 5 + .5*Qs

Use values for quantity (Q) from $0 to 130 in increments of 10. Place this information in the input area of your solution sheet and calculate the price for each quantity data point from the demand relationship (P(Qd)). Note: this result answers the question "in order to sell each of these quantities, what is the highest price that could be charged based on consumer demand for this good?"

Similarly, calculate the price for each quantity data point from the supply relationship (P(Qs)). Note: this result answers the question "in order to obtain a supply to the market for this good in each of the quantities, what is the minimum price that could be offered to suppliers based on producer supply for this good?"

c. Construct a line chart showing the market demand and supply from the data you calculated in part b for P(Qd) and P(Qs), labeling this data D and S respectively. Use the quantity data as the x-axis.

d.   Using the supply and demand curves constructed, determine the market equilibrium price and quantity. Compare the results with the values calculated in part a.

4.   CHANGE IN DEMAND*

a.   Construct a worksheet with a column of prices from $0 to $100 in increments of $10. Compute the quantity demanded (Qd) and quantity supplied (Qs) for each of these prices using the following formulas:
$$Qd = 165 - .6*P$$
$$Qs = -37.50 + .75*P$$

b.   Prepare a line chart of the quantity demanded and quantity supplied. In order to do this you, must rewrite the formulas to show the relationship in terms of price being a function of quantity. Note: Create additional columns showing quantity (Q), the price at each quantity demanded (P(Qd)) and price at each quantity supplied (P(Qs)). Use values for Q from 0 to 175 in increments of 25. The inverse of the demand and supply relationships are:
$$P(Qd) = 275 - (5/3)*Qd$$
$$P(Qs) = 50 + (4/3)*Qs$$
(where Qd and Qs are Q)
Label these D and S respectively and use the quantity data as the x-axis. What is the equilibrium price and quantity?

c.   Suppose the formula for P(Qd) changes to: P(Qd)=200 - (5/3)*Qd
What is the new equilibrium price and quantity? (Note: insert the new formula into your existing worksheet in order to find out the answer.)

5.   CHANGE IN DEMAND

a.   Prepare a worksheet with a column for quantity ranging from 0 to 130 in increments of 10. Use the formulas shown below to calculate P(Qd) and P(Qs).
Input Area:

Q	P(Qd)	P(Qs)
0	=55-.5*Qd	=5+.5*Qs
10		
20		
|		
130		

P(Qd) is the market demand relationship expressed as price being a function of quantity. P(Qs) is the market supply relationship expressed as price being a function of quantity.

b.   Add to your input area another market demand relationship: $P'(Qd) = 65-.5*Q$
Calculate the price values for each quantity data point using the demand relationship ($P(Qd)$), the supply relationship ($P(Qs)$), and the additional demand relationship ($P'(Qd)$).

c.   Construct a line chart of the price data for all three of these relationships. Label them D, S, and D' respectively. Use the quantity data as the x-axis.

d.   What would the market equilibrium be for $P(Qd)=D$ and $P(Qs)=S$? D' represents a new market demand or a shift in the demand curve (called a change in demand). What would the new market equilibrium be for $P'(Qd)=D'$ and $P(Qs)=S$?

e.   Is D' an increase or a decrease in market demand? How do you know? What would happen to market equilibrium if equilibrium demand shifted to the left? Would this be an increase or decrease in demand?

6.   CHANGE IN SUPPLY

a.   Prepare a worksheet with a column for quantity ranging from 0 to 130 in increments of 10. Use the formulas shown below to calculate $P(Qd)$ and $P(Qs)$.
Input Area:

Q	P(Qd)	P(Qs)
0	=55-.5*Qd	=5+.5*Qs
10		
20		
│		
130		

$P(Qd)$ is the market demand relationship expressed as price being a function of quantity. $P(Qs)$ is the market supply relationship expressed as price being a function of quantity.

Add to your input area another market supply relationship: $P'(Qs)=25+.5*Qs$
Calculate the price values for each demand relationship ($P(Qd)$) and both supply relationships ($P(Qs)$ and $P'(Qs)$).

b.   Construct a line chart of the price data for all three of these relationships. Label them D, S, and S' respectively. Use the quantity data as the x-axis.

c.   What would the market equilibrium be for $P(Qd)=D$ and $P(Qs)=S$? S represents a new market supply curve (called a change in supply). After supply changes to S', at the original equilibrium price what is the shortage or surplus in the market?

d. What will the new market equilibrium be for demand D and supply S'? Is this an increase or decrease in supply? What would happen to equilibrium price and quantity if supply were to shift to the right? Would this represent an increase or decrease in supply?

7. CHANGE IN BOTH DEMAND AND SUPPLY

When either demand or supply changes in a market, we are able to be certain of the direction of change of both the equilibrium price and quantity even without knowing the exact magnitude of the change. When both change simultaneously, we are limited to being able to predict the direction of change of either price or quantity depending on whether both changed in the same direction (both increase or both decrease) or they change in opposite directions (one increases as the other decreases).

a. Using the data provided below, construct a worksheet in order to show the impact of a simultaneous change in both market demand and supply. Calculate the price data at each quantity (Q) point for P(Qd), P(Qs), P'(Qd), and P'(Qs). The column of quantity should range from 0 to 130 in increments of 10.
Input Area:

Q(Qd or Qs)	P(Qd)	P(Qs)	P'(Qd)	P'(Qs)
0	=55-.5*Qd	=5+.5*Qs	=65-.5*Qd	=15+.5*Qs
10				
20				
130				

b. Construct a line chart of the data for P(Qd), P(Qs), P'(Qd), and P'(Qs). Label them D, S, D', and S', respectively. Use the quantity (Q) data for the x-axis.

c. Has demand increased or decreased? Has supply increased or decreased? What has happened to the equilibrium price? What has happened to the equilibrium quantity? Suppose that demand and supply have changed in the opposite directions demonstrated and by exactly the same amount (D' to D and S' to S). What would have happened to the equilibrium price and quantity? When demand and supply change in opposite directions, for which variable (price or quantity) are we certain of the direction of change?

d. Suppose demand has started out at D' and changed to D as supply changed from S to S'. What would have happened to the market equilibrium? Which variable is predictable regarding the direction of change whenever demand and supply change in the same direction (both increase or both decrease)?

8.   PRICE ELASTICITY OF DEMAND*

The price elasticity of demand, PE(D), is computed by dividing the percent change in quantity demanded by the percent change in price. Alternatively, the PE(D) can be computed at any given price (P) by dividing that price by the negative of the difference of the vertical axis intercept less price. The formula is as follows:

PE(D) = (P) / (P - VID)

Where: PE(D) is the price elasticity of demand.
                     VID is the vertical axis intercept of the demand curve.
                     P is the price (corresponding to a specific quantity demanded).

a.   Construct a worksheet using the data provided below. The equation for quantity demanded is: Qd=155-1*P. Restated in terms of price, it is: P(Qd)=155-1*Qd. Use values for quantity ranging from 0 to 140 in increments of 10. The VID is 155; thus, at a price of 155, quantity demanded is 0. Note: Delete data in cells where formulas do not work due to division by 0 or missing reference data.

Input Area:

Qd	P(Qd)	Q	PE(D)	TR	MR
=155-P	=155-Q	0	=P/(P-VID)	=P*Q	=((P_{i+1}*Q_{i+1})-(P_i*Q_i))/(Q_{i+1}-Q_i)
		10		or	or change in TR/change in Q
		20		=(155-Q)*Q	
		|		=155Q-Q^2	
		140		=155*Q-Q^2	

PE(D) = P/(P-VID) where VID is the vertical intercept of demand function written as P being a function of Q or P(Qd)=155-Q, =155 (intercept is (155,0), when Qd=0, P=155).

b.   Create a line chart showing P(Qd), MR, and PE(D). Note: To create the chart, you may rearrange your columns so that the columns containing P(Qd), MR, and PE(D) are side by side, making them easier to highlight. *Charting hint*: Paint in the data to be graphed, that is, the values for P(Qd), MR, and PE(D). Click on the Chart Wizard icon. In step 1, select "Line" chart. In step 2, select "Series" and enter the range for the x-axis labels, in this case the range corresponding to values for Qd. To make the x-axis and y-axis cross at zero, you must click on the x-axis, which brings up the "Format axis" menu box. Next, click on the "Scale" tab and un-check the box labeled "Value (y) axis crosses between categories."

9.   PRICE ELASTICITY OF DEMAND

The price elasticity of demand, PE(D), is computed by dividing the percent change in quantity demanded by the percent change in price. Alternatively, the PE(D) can be computed at any given price (P) by dividing that price by the negative of the difference of the vertical axis intercept less price. The formula is as follows:

$PE(D) = (P) / (P - VID)$

Where: PE(D) is the price elasticity of demand.

VID is the vertical axis intercept of the demand curve.

P is the price (corresponding to a specific quantity demanded).

a. Construct a worksheet with the data provided below. The output area should contain Q, P(Qd), TR, MR, and PE(D). The equation for quantity demanded is Q(d)=15-1*P. This can be restated as P(Qd)=15-Q. Quantity should range from 0 to 15 in increments of one.

Input Area:

Qd	P(Qd)	Q	PE(D)	TR	MR
=15-P	=15-Q	0	=P/(P-VID)	=P*Q	=$((P_{i+1}*Q_{i+1})-(P_i*Q_i))/(Q_{i+1}-Q_i)$
		1		or	or change in TR/change in Q
		2		=(15-Q)*Q	
		|		=$15Q-Q^2$	
		15		=15*Q-Q^2	

PE(D) = P/(P-VID) where VID is the vertical intercept of demand function written as P being a function of Q, or P(Qd)=15-Q, =15 (intercept is (15,0), when Qd=0, P=15)

b. Create a line chart showing P(Qd), TR, MR, and PE(D). Note: To create the chart, you can rearrange your columns so that the columns containing P(Qd), TR, MR, and PE(D) are side by side, making them easier to highlight.

Charting hint: Paint in the data to be graphed, that is, the values for P(Qd), TR, MR, and PE(D). Click on the Chart Wizard icon. In step 1, select "Line" chart. In step 2, select "Series" and enter the range for the x-axis labels, in this case the range corresponding to values for Qd. To make the x-axis and y-axis cross at zero, you must click on the x-axis, which brings up the "Format axis" menu box. Next, click on the "Scale" tab and un-check the box labeled "Value (y) axis crosses between categories." Refer to Chapter 4 if you need more directions.

10.   INCOME ELASTICITY OF DEMAND

Income is a primary determining factor in the demand for goods and services. A significant change in income can change the quantities of a good sold at every price. If the quantity demanded at every price increases as income increases, it is considered a "normal" good. Some goods exhibit an inverse relationship between changes in income and quantity demanded at each price. These goods are called "inferior." As income increases, inferior goods are substituted for more costly but preferred alternatives. The effect of income on market demand for a good is measured using the income elasticity of demand (IE(D)). This number shows the strength of income changes on quantity demanded and if the effect is direct (normal) or inverse (inferior).

a.   Construct a worksheet using the following data.

Input Area:

P	Q or Qd	Q' or Q'd	% chY	IE(D)	P'
$55	0		.1	=%chQd / %chY	$55.00
50	10			where Y=income	50.24
45	20			or =((Q-Q')/Q) / %chY	45.48
40	30	31.5			40.72
35	40				35.96
30	50				31.20
25	60				26.44
20	70				21.68
15	80				16.92
10	90				12.16
5	100				7.40
0	110				2.64

Q is the quantity data.

P is the corresponding price data for a good at the original income level.

Q' or Q'd represents the quantity that would be demanded at the prices P after income changed. As you can see, we only have one observation: at a price of $40 the original quantity demanded was 30; and after income changed, it was 31.5.

%chY represents the percentage change in income as a decimal. In this case, .1 represents an increase in income of 10%.

IE(D) is the income elasticity of demand. IE(D) = (%chQd) / (%chY) where Y is income.

P' represents the predicted prices consumers would be willing to pay to purchase the original quantities Q at the new income level given the income elasticity of demand.

b.   Calculate the IE(D). Hint: There is one observation of the change in quantity which can be used to calculate the percentage change in Qd for a given percentage change in income.

c.   Calculate the missing data for Q' or Qd' using the IE(D) relationship (the IE(D) value calculated in part b) and solving for Q. We know IE(D)=((Q-Q')/Q)/%chY, if we solve for Q' we find Q'=Q+(Q*IE(D)*%chY). In this way, one can predict the quantities demanded at the original price points given the change in demand due to the change in income, assuming that IE(D) is a constant for all price levels.

d.   Construct a line chart of the data for P and P'. Label them D and D', respectively. Use the original quantity data, Q or Qd, as the x-axis.

e.   Is this good a normal or inferior good? Explain. What would have happened to the demand for this good if income had fallen rather than increased?

11. INCOME ELASTICITY OF DEMAND

a. Construct a worksheet using the data provided below. The column of quantity (Q or Qd) should range from 0 to 110 in increments of 10. Calculate the quantities consumers will demand at the original prices after income has changed (Q'). Calculate the prices consumers would be willing to pay for the original quantities (Q or Qd) after income has changed: P'(Qd)

Input Area:

Qd(P)	P(Qd)	Q	IE(D)	%chY	Q' or Q'd	P'(Qd)
=110-2*P	=55-.5*Q	0	2	.05	=Q+(Q*IE(D)*%chY)	=55-.45*Qd
		10				
		20				
		|				
		110				

IE(D) is the income elasticity of demand. IE(D) = (%chQd) / (%chY) where Y is income.

%chY is the percentage change in Y expressed as a decimal.

.05 represents a 5% increase in income.

Q' or Qd' represents the quantity demanded for this good at the original prices after the change in income.

P'(Qd) represents the relationship that results in the prices consumers would be willing to pay for the original quantities (Q or Qd) after the effects of the change in income have been included in the demand for this good.

b. What happened to the quantities demanded after the income change (Q') compared to the original quantities (Q) demanded at each of these prices?

c. Construct a line chart of the data for P(Qd) and P'(Qd) and label them D and D', respectively. Use the quantity data Q for the x-axis. These curves represent the demand for this good at the original income and the demand after income changed.

d. Is this good a normal or inferior good? Explain. Are the demand curves D and D' consistent with the income change and income elasticity of demand for this good? Explain. If the IE(D) for this good had been a negative number, what would have happened to demand for this income change?

12. CROSS PRICE ELASTICITY OF DEMAND

The prices of related goods (substitutes and compliments) affect the demand for a given good. We measure the direction (direct or inverse) and magnitude of the effects using cross price elasticity of demand (CPE(D)). Similar to other types of elasticity, we calculate CPE(D) as percentage change in quantity demanded of a given good divided by the percentage change in the price of a related good. Knowing the effects that changes in price of substitutes and compliments have on demand, we can reason what the sign of the CPE(D) for each would be.

a. Using the data provided below, construct a worksheet to demonstrate the effect of a change in the price of a related good on the demand for a given good. The column of quantity should range from 0 to 110 in increments of 10. Calculate the price of the good based on the original demand relationship for each quantity (Q) point and for the subsequent demand relationship (P'(Qd)). Given the original market price, determine the quantity demanded before and after the demand change.

Input Area:

Q(also Qd)	P(Qd)	CPE(D)	P	%ch in Pr	P'(Qd)
0	=55-.5*Qd	=(%ch in Qd)/(%ch in Pr)	$30	.2	=55-.65*Qd
10					
20					
110					

CPE(D) is the cross price elasticity of demand.
P is the market price for the good under consideration.
%ch in Pr is the percentage change in the price of a related good (Pr).
P'(Qd) is the change in demand that occurs as a result of the change in the price of the related good.

b. Construct a line chart for the price data for P(Qd) and P'(Qd). Label them D and D', respectively. Use the quantity (Q) data for the x-axis.

c. Calculate the percentage change in the quantity demanded and divide it by the percentage change in the price of the related good (%ch in Pr) in order to calculate the CPE(D). What is the cross price elasticity of demand? Is this a direct or an inverse relationship? What type of relationship exists between these goods?

d. Suppose instead of rising by 20% (%ch in Pr = .2), the price of the related good had fallen significantly. What would be expected to happen to the demand for the good?

13. CROSS PRICE ELASTICITY OF DEMAND

The prices of related goods (substitutes and compliments) affect the demand for a given good. We measure the direction (direct or inverse) and magnitude of the effects using cross price elasticity of demand (CPE(D)). Similar to other types of elasticity, we calculate CPE(D) as percentage change in quantity demanded of a given good divided by the percentage change in the price of a related good. Knowing the effects that changes in price of substitutes and compliments have on demand, we can reason what the sign of the CPE(D) for each would be.

a.   Using the data provided below, construct a worksheet to demonstrate the effect of a change in the price of a related good on the demand for a given good. The column of quantity should range from 0 to 110 in increments of 10. Calculate the price of the good based on the original demand relationship for each quantity (Q) point and for the subsequent demand relationship (P'(Qd)). Given the original market price, determine the quantity demanded before and after the demand change.

Input Area:

Q(or Qd)	P(Qd)	CPE(D)	P	%ch in Pr	P'(Qd)
0	=55-.5*Q	=(%ch in Qd)/(%ch in Pr)	$35	.1	=55-.4*Qd
10					
20					
|					
110					

CPE(D) is the cross price elasticity of demand.
P is the market price for the good under consideration.
%ch in Pr is the percentage change in the price of a related good (Pr).
P'(Qd) is the change in demand that occurs as a result of the change in the price of the related good.

b.   Construct a line chart for the price data for P(Qd) and P'(Qd). Label them D and D', respectively. Use the quantity (Q) data for the x-axis.

c.   Calculate the percentage change in the quantity demanded and divide it by the percentage change in the price of the related good (%ch in Pr) in order to calculate the CPE(D). What is the cross price elasticity of demand? Is this a direct or inverse relationship? What type of relationship exists between these goods?

d.   Suppose instead of rising by 10% (%ch in Pr = .1), the price of the related good had fallen significantly. What would be expected to happen to the demand for the good?

14.   PRICE ELASTICITY OF SUPPLY

The price elasticity of supply (PE(S)), is computed by dividing the percent change in quantity supplied by the percent change in price. Alternatively, the PE(S) can be computed at any given price (P) by dividing that price by the price less the vertical axis intercept. The formula is as follows:

$$PE(S) = (P) / (P - VIS)$$

Where: PE(S) is the price elasticity of supply.

                      VIS is the vertical axis intercept of the supply curve.

                      P is the price (corresponding to a specific quantity supplied).

Use the following equation for quantity supplied: $Qs = -1 + 1*P$. The equation can be restated as: $P(Qs) = 1 + 1*Q$ (the inverse, or price as a function of quantity supplied).

a.   Prepare a worksheet showing P, Qs, P(Qs), Q, and PE(S). Use values for quantity from 0 to 15 in increments of one. Use values for market price of $0 to $100 in increments of $10. Note: The VIS is one. Thus, when P = 1, Qs = 0. Note: After entering formulas, an error message will appear in the first row of PE(S) saying that division by zero is not allowed (#DIV/0!). If preferred, this cell may be deleted for appearance sake; otherwise, PE(S) will be charted as having a value of zero at quantity of zero.

b.   Construct a line chart showing P(Qs) and PE(S). Hint: Paint in the data to be graphed, that is, the values for P(Qs) and PE(S). Click on the Chart Wizard icon. In step 1, select "Line" chart. In step 2, select "Series" and enter the range for x-axis labels, in this case the range containing values of Qs.

15.   PRICE ELASTICITY OF SUPPLY

The price elasticity of supply (PE(S)), is computed by dividing the percent change in quantity supplied by the percent change in price. Alternatively, the PE(S) can be computed at any given price (P) by dividing that price by the price less the vertical axis intercept. The formula is as follows:

        PE(S) = (P) / (P - VIS)

        Where: PE(S) is the price elasticity coefficient of supply.

                        VIS is the vertical axis intercept of the supply curve.

                        P is the price (corresponding to a specific quantity supplied).

Use the following equation for quantity supplied: $Qs = 1 + .5*P$. The equation can be restated as: $P(Qs) = 2 + 2*Q$ (the inverse, or price as a function of quantity supplied).

a.   Prepare a worksheet showing P, Qs, P(Qs), Q, and PE(S). Use values for quantity from 0 to 15 in increments of one. Use values for market price of $0 to $100 in increments of $10. Note: The VIS is 2. Thus, when P = 2, Qs = 0. Note: After entering formulas, an error message will appear in the first row of PE(S) saying that division by zero is not allowed (#DIV/0!). If preferred, this cell may be deleted for appearance sake; otherwise, PE(S) will be charted as having a value of zero at quantity of zero.

b.   Construct a line chart showing P(Qs) and PE(S). Hint: Paint in the data to be graphed, that is, the values for P(Qs) and PE(S). Click on the Chart Wizard icon.

In step 1, select "Line" chart. In step 2, select "Series" and enter the range for x-axis labels, in this case the range containing values of Qs.

16.   INDIFFERENCE CURVES*

a.   Construct a worksheet using the information provided below showing quantity combinations for two goods (good A and good B) providing a consumer identical levels of satisfaction (Utility). This means that the consumer is indifferent to which of the combinations he or she chooses among the sets that result in the same level of satisfaction.

Input Area:

Q(B)	$Q(A)@I_1$:	$Q(A)@I_2$
0		
4	46	60
8	22	30
12	9	16
16	4	7.5
20	3.4	5
24	2.9	4.3
28	2.5	3.8
32	2.2	3.5
36	2	3.3
40	1.9	3.2

Q(B) represents the quantity of good B.
Q(A) represents the quantity of good A.
I_1 indicates a level of consumer satisfaction (or utility).
I_2 represents a level of satisfaction greater than I_1.
$Q(A)@I_1$ represents a quantity of good A in combination with the corresponding quantity of good B (Q(B)) resulting in I_1 level of satisfaction.
$Q(A)@I_2$ indicates the quantity of good a required for I_2 level of satisfaction for each of the quantities of good B.

Note: Based on the assumption of increasing utility for additional units of good A for a given quantity of good B, I_2 level of utility is greater than I_1 level of utility.

b.   Construct a line chart for I_1 and I_2 using the given data for $Q(A)@I_1$ and $Q(A)@I_2$. Use the quantity data for good B as the x-axis.

c.   Why is it reasonable to believe that I_2 represents a higher level of utility than I_1?

d.   What principle of indifference curves does the shape of I_1 and I_2 demonstrate that is closely related to diminishing marginal utility?

17.   BUDGET CONSTRAINT

a.   Construct a worksheet using the following information showing quantity combinations for two goods (good A and good B) providing a consumer identical levels of satisfaction (utility). Included are the market prices for goods A and B (P(A) and P(B)), the budget of the consumer (Y), and the budget constraint relationship (Y(A,B)). Calculate the quantity of good A (Q(A)) at each specified level of good B using the budget constraint (Y(A,B)).

Input area:

Q(B)	Q(A)@I_1	Q(A)@I_2	P(A)	P(B)	Y	Y(A,B)
0			$20	$5	$200	=(Q(A)*P(A))+(Q(B)*P(B))
4	46	60				or
8	22	30				
12	9	16				Q(A)=(200/P(A))-((Q(B)*P(B))/P(A))
16	4	7.5				
20	3.2	5				
24	2.8	4.3				
28	2.4	3.8				
32	2.1	3.5				
36	2	3.3				
40	1.9	3.2				

b.   Construct a line chart for the indifference quantities of good A for each of the specified levels of good B at indifference level 1 (Q(A)@I_1), the same for Q(A)@I_2 and the quantities of good A for each of the specified levels of good B as indicated by the budget constraint (Y(A,B)). Use data for the quantity of good B (Q(B)) as the x-axis. Label Q(A)@I_1 as I_1, Q(A)@I_2 as I_2 and Y(A,B) as Y(A,B).

c.   At what quantities of good A and good B will the consumer attain his or her maximum utility given the budget constraint (line) Y(A,B)?

d.   Using I_1 as an example of a lower indifference curve, explain why other combinations of good A and good B along the budget line would result in lower utility for the consumer than the maximum utility combination stated in part c.

18.   PRICE CHANGE EFFECT ON BUDGET CONSTRAINT

a.   Construct a worksheet using the information provided below showing quantity combinations for two goods (good A and good B) providing a consumer identical levels of satisfaction (utility). [(Q(B), Q(A)@I_1) and Q(B), Q(A)@I_2)] Included are the market prices for goods A and B (P(A) and P(B)) and the budget constraint relationship. Additionally, a new budget for the consumer and market price for good A is provided (P'(A)). Calculate the quantity of good A at each level of good B using the budget constraint relationship (Y'(A,B)) with the price of good A as P(A). Calculate the quantity of good A at each level of good B using the budget constraint relationship with the new price of good A (P'(A)). Label this as Y'(A,B).

Input area:

Q(B)	Q(A)@I_1	Q(A)@I_2	P(A)	P(B)	P'(A)'	Y	Y(A,B)	Y'(A,B)
0			$20	$5	$12	$160		
4	46	60						
8	22	30						
12	9	16						
16	4	7.5						
20	3.2	5						
24	2.8	4.3						
28	2.4	3.8						
32	2.1	3.5						
36	2	3.3						
40	1.9	3.2						

$$Y(A,B) = (Q(A)*P(A)) + (Q(B)*P(B)) \quad or \quad Q(A) = (200/P(A)) - ((Q(B)*P(B))/P(A))$$

b. Construct a line chart for the indifference quantities of good A for each of the specified levels of good B at indifference level 1 (Q(A)@I_1) and indifference level 2 (Q(A)@I_2) and the quantities of good A for each of the specified levels of good B as indicated by the budget constraints (Y(A,B) and Y'(A,B)).

c. What is the effect of a price reduction of one good on the quantities the consumer can purchase of the two goods?

d. What is the effect on the level of satisfaction the consumer gets from his or her fixed budget?

e. Observe the combinations of quantities that this consumer will choose at a variety of different prices for good A by determining the point of tangency between the budget lines that results from the price changes and his or her indifference curves. What can be derived from knowing these combinations of P(A) and Q(A)?

19.   UTILITY ANALYSIS*

Use the following equations to determine the quantities of product A and product B to purchase in order to maximize total utility. Note, in Excel the "^" is used to designate an exponent, in this case the exponent 2 or "squared" (^2).

Total utility of product A: $TU(A) = 105*Q(A) - 5*Q(A)^2$
                                or $=105*Q(A)-5*Q(A)^2$

Average utility of product A:	AU(A) = 105 - 5*Q(A)
Marginal utility of product A:	MU(A) = 105 - 10*Q(A)
Unit price of A:	P(A) = $5
Total utility of product B:	TU(B) = 42*Q(B) - 2*Q(B)^2
	or =42*Q(B)-2*Q(B)^2
Average utility of product B:	AU(B) = 42 - 2*Q(B)
Marginal utility of product B:	MU(B) = 42 - 4*Q(B)
Unit price of B:	P(B) = $10

a.   Construct a worksheet showing quantities of A and B, total utility and marginal utility of each, as well as marginal utilities of each divided by the respective prices. Show quantities of A and B from 0 to 11 in increments of 1 unit.

b.   If you have $75 to spend (your income or budget limit), how much of each product would you buy to maximize your total utility? Why would this be the best way to maximize your utility from buying these two goods with your total budget of $75? What rule was used?

c.   Prepare the following line charts:
  • TU(A)
  • MU(A) divided by P(A)
  • TU(B)
  • MU(B) divided by P(B)

How do the marginal utility per dollar charts show that the quantity selected for each good is the best that can be done with $75?

20.   UTILITY ANALYSIS - DERIVING A DEMAND CURVE

a.   Using the information from the previous assignment, determine the impact on MU(A) / P(A) based on prices for A of $5, $10, $15, and $20. Add columns to the worksheet for MU(A) / P(A) where P(A) = $5, $10, $15, and $20. Determine the quantity demanded for good A at each price given.

b.   Prepare a line chart of the demand curve for Product A. Note: The data will not reflect a price when the quantity is zero. In order to obtain a chart that depicts the origin (0,0), you must specify the x-axis data with a zero as the first point in the data series and the y-axis data as having a blank data cell as the first point in the data series.

21.   PRODUCTION FUNCTION*

The production function is the relationship that relates the quantity of inputs (or factors of production) to the output of the firm's product. It is common for some inputs (such as labor) to be variable in the short run while some factors (such as capital) are fixed in the short run.

a. Construct a worksheet based on the data provided below.
   Input Area:

Q(A)	Q(B)	TPP	Q'(A)	TPP'
40	0	0	50	0
	5	5		5.5
	10	11		12
	15	20		21.5
	20	33.5		36
	25	49		54
	30	63		70
	35	73		83
	40	80		92
	45	85		99
	50	88		102.5
	55	90		105
	60	91		106.5
	65	90		107

Q(A) is the quantity of a fixed factor (A).
Q(B) is the quantity of the variable factor (B).
TPP stands for total physical product and is the output resulting from various combinations of the fixed factor A and variable quantities of factor B.

In the long run, the firm is free to choose a different quantity of the fixed factor, but once it is obtained, it is again fixed in the short term. Q'(A) indicates a different quantity of factor A and TPP' represents the output of the firm with the increased quantity of factor A (Q'(A)) in combination with the same quantities of factor B (Q(B)).

b. Construct a line chart using the data from TPP and TPP'. Use the data for the quantity of factor B as the x-axis.

c. Why does the production function reach some maximum output in the short run as the variable factor is increased? At what level of Q(B) does TPP reach its maximum?

d. If production is reconfigured with more of the fixed factor A, what would likely happen to output at any level of the variable factor B?

e. What would happen to the quantity of the variable factor B where the production function would reach its maximum?

22.   TOTAL AND MARGINAL PRODUCT*

Total product (or total physical product) is the output of the firm's product that results from the use of factors of production or inputs. Marginal product (or marginal physical product) is the measure of the change in output for a change in the quantity of an input. It tells us what will happen to total output if we change the use of a factor by a unit.

a.   Construct a worksheet using the following data. Calculate the marginal physical product from the variable factor quantities and total product provided.
Input Area:

Q(A)	Q(B)	TPP	MPP
40	0	0	$=(TPP_i-TPP_{i-1})/(Q(B)_i-Q(B)_{i-1})$
	5	5	
	10	11	
	15	20	
	20	33.5	
	25	49	
	30	63	
	35	73	
	40	80	
	45	85	
	50	88	
	55	90	
	60	91	
	65	90	

Q(A)   is the quantity of a fixed factor (A).
Q(B)   is the quantity of the variable factor (B).
TPP   stands for total physical product and is the output resulting from various combinations of the fixed factor A and variable quantities of factor B.
MPP   stands for marginal physical product. Marginal product is defined as the change in output divided by the change in the variable factor. The relationship is provided as a formula and represented by MPP.

b.   What do you notice about the MPP when Q(B) is 65?

c.   Construct two separate line charts and place them side-by-side in comparison. Construct a line chart for the TPP data. Use the quantity data for factor B (Q(B)) as the x-axis. Construct a line chart for the MPP data. Use the quantity data for factor B as the x-axis.

d.   Suppose production is at an output level 33.5 where 20 units of the variable factor B are being used. Should output remain at this level, given what the MPP data reveals? What is noticeable about MPP in the range of variable factor use from 0 to 25?

e. What is noticeable about MPP in the range of variable factor use from 25 to 60?

23. PRODUCTION ANALYSIS

a. Construct a worksheet using the data provided. Calculate MPP, and APP.
Input Area:

Q(A)	Q(B)	TPP	MPP	APP
40	0	0	$=(TPP_i-TPP_{i-1})/(Q(B)_i-Q(B)_{i-1})$	$=TPP/Q(B)$
	5	5		
	10	11		
	15	20		
	20	33.5		
	25	49		
	30	63		
	35	73		
	40	80		
	45	85		
	50	88		
	55	90		
	60	91		
	65	90		

Q(A) is the quantity of a fixed factor (A).
Q(B) is the quantity of the variable factor (B).
TPP stands for total physical product and is the output resulting from
combinations of the fixed factor A and variable quantities of factor B.
MPP stands for marginal physical product. Marginal product is defined as the
change in output divided by the change in the variable factor. The
relationship is provided as a formula and represented by MPP.
APP is the average physical product. APP is computed by dividing TPP by Q(B).

Note: Delete data in cells where formulas do not work due to division by zero or missing reference data.

b. Prepare a line chart showing the production function (i.e., TPP). Use quantities of Q(B) as the x-axis. Refer to the charting hint in assignment 16.

c. Prepare a line chart of MPP and APP. Use quantities of Q(B) as the x-axis. Refer to the charting hint in assignment 16.

24. TOTAL COST ANALYSIS

a.   Construct a worksheet using the following data. Calculate total fixed cost (TFC), total variable cost (TVC), and total cost (TC).

Input Area:

Q(A)	P(A)	Q(B)	P(B)	TPP	TFC	TVC	TC
30	$50	0	$100	0	=P(A)*Q(A)	=P(B)*Q(B)	=TFC+TVC
		6		10			
		11		20			
		15		30			
		18		40			
		20		50			
		23		60			
		27		70			
		33		80			
		41		90			
		52		100			
		66		110			
		87		120			

Q(A) is quantity of the fixed factor A.
Q(B) is quantity of the variable factor B.
P(A) is price of factor A, the fixed input.
P(B) is price of factor B, the variable input.
TPP stands for total physical product and is the output resulting from various combinations of the fixed factor A and variable quantities of factor B.
TFC is total fixed cost.
TVC is total variable cost.
TC is total cost.

Note: Delete data in cells where formulas will not work due to either division by 0 or cell references are lacking values.

b.   Prepare a line chart showing TFC, TVC, and TC. Use values of TPP as the x-axis. Refer to the charting hint in assignment 16.

25. UNIT COST ANALYSIS

Note: The data used in this assignment originated in assignment 24.

a.   Construct a worksheet with the data provided below. Calculate average fixed cost (AFC), average variable cost (AVC), average total cost (ATC), and marginal cost (MC).

Input Area:

Q(A)	Q(B)	TPP	TFC	TVC	TC	AFC	AVC	ATC	MC
30	0	0	$1500	$ 0	$1500	=TFC/TPP	=TVC/TPP	=TC/TPP	
	6	10	1500	600	2100				
	11	20	1500	1100	2600				
	15	30	1500	1500	3000				
	18	40	1500	1800	3300				
	20	50	1500	2000	3500				
	23	60	1500	2300	3800				
	27	70	1500	2700	4200				
	33	80	1500	3300	4800				
	41	90	1500	4100	5600				
	52	100	1500	5200	6700				
	66	110	1500	6600	8100				
	87	120	1500	8700	10200				

MC $= (TC_i - TC_{i-1})/(TPP_i - TPP_{i-1})$. MC represents marginal cost.

b.   Prepare a line chart showing the unit costs functions: AFC, AVC, ATC, and MC. Use the values of TPP as the x-axis. Refer to the charting hint in assignment 16.

26.   UNIT COST AND REVENUE ANALYSIS*

a.   Starting with the following input data (which was created in assignment 25), add columns (with formulas) for price of good Y (P(Y)), total revenue (TR), and marginal revenue (MR). Calculate TR and MR for each total physical product (TPP) point. The P(Y) value will be incorporated into the total revenue relationship. Since P(Y) is a constant at all levels of output, the demand curve for this firm (and average revenue curve) is horizontal and P(Y)=AR=MR. This firm is a price taker or a pure competitor.

TPP	AFC	AVC	ATC	MC	P(Y)	TR	MR
0					$60	=P(Y)*TPP	$= (TR_i - TR_{i-1})/(TPP_i - TPP_{i-1})$
10	$150.00	$60.00	$210.00	$60			
20	75.00	55.00	130.00	50			
30	50.00	50.00	100.00	40			
40	37.50	45.00	82.50	30			
50	30.00	40.00	70.00	20			
60	25.00	38.33	63.33	30			
70	21.43	38.57	60.00	40			
80	18.75	41.25	60.00	60			
90	16.66	45.56	62.22	80			
100	15.00	52.00	67.00	110			
110	13.64	60.00	73.64	140			
120	12.50	72.50	85.00	210			

b.   Construct a line chart of the AFC, AVC, ATC, MC and MR data. Label them appropriately. Use the TPP data for the x-axis and label it quantity of output.

c.   What output would this firm choose to produce and how would this output be determined?

d.   WHAT IF the price of good Y (P(Y)) increased to $80. Put this data into the worksheet and determine the firm's optimum output.

27.   UNIT COST AND REVENUE ANALYSIS

a.   Starting with the following data (which was created in assignment 25), add columns (with formulas) for price of good Y (P(Y)), total revenue (TR), and marginal revenue (MR). Calculate TR and MR for each total physical product (TPP) point. The P(Y) value will be incorporated into the total revenue relationship. Since P(Y) is a constant at all levels of output, the demand curve for this firm (and average revenue curve) is horizontal and P(Y)=AR=MR. This firm is a price taker or a pure competitor.

Input Area:

TPP	AFC	AVC	ATC	MC	P(Y)	TR	MR
0					$50	=P(Y)*TPP	=(TR$_i$-TR$_{i-1}$)/(TPP$_i$-TPP$_{i-1}$)
10	$150.00	$60.00	$210.00	$60			
20	75.00	55.00	130.00	50			
30	50.00	50.00	100.00	40			
40	37.50	45.00	82.50	30			
50	30.00	40.00	70.00	20			
60	25.00	38.33	63.33	30			
70	21.43	38.57	60.00	40			
80	18.75	41.25	60.00	60			
90	16.67	45.56	62.22	80			
100	15.00	52.00	67.00	110			
110	13.64	60.00	73.64	140			
120	12.50	72.50	85.00	210			

b.   Construct a line chart of the AFC, AVC, ATC, MC and MR data. Use the TPP data for the x-axis and label it quantity of output.

c.   What output would this firm choose to produce and how would this output be determined?

d.   WHAT IF the price of good Y (P(Y)) increased to $70. Put this data into the worksheet and determine the firm's optimum output.

28. UNIT COST AND REVENUE ANALYSIS

Note: This data is similar to assignment 26 except that the price of good Y (P(Y)) is decreased to $40.

a.   Starting with the following data (which was created in assignment 25), add columns (with formulas) for price of good Y (P(Y)), total revenue (TR), and marginal revenue (MR). Calculate TR and MR for each total physical product (TPP) point. The P(Y) value will be incorporated into the total revenue relationship. Since P(Y) is a constant at all levels of output, the demand curve for this firm (and average revenue curve) is horizontal and P(Y)=AR=MR. This firm is a price taker or a pure competitor.

Input Area:

TPP	AFC	AVC	ATC	MC	P(Y)	TR	MR
0					$40	=P(Y)*TPP	=(TR$_i$-TR$_{i-1}$)/(TPP$_i$-TPP$_{i-1}$)
10	$150.00	$60.00	$210.00	$60			
20	75.00	55.00	130.00	50			
30	50.00	50.00	100.00	40			
40	37.50	45.00	82.50	30			
50	30.00	40.00	70.00	20			
60	25.00	38.33	63.33	30			
70	21.43	38.57	60.00	40			
80	18.75	41.25	60.00	60			
90	16.67	45.56	62.22	80			
100	15.00	52.00	67.00	110			
110	13.64	60.00	73.64	140			
120	12.50	72.50	85.00	210			

b.   Construct a line chart of the AFC, AVC, ATC, MC and MR data. Label them appropriately. Use the TPP data for the x-axis and label it quantity of output.

c.   What output would this firm choose to produce and how would this output be determined?

d.   WHAT IF the price of good Y (P(Y)) decreased to $30. Put this data into the worksheet and determine the firm's optimum output.

29. UNIT COST AND REVENUE ANALYSIS

a.   Create a worksheet using the following data, including columns (with formulas) for price of good Y (P(Y)), total revenue (TR), and marginal revenue (MR). Calculate average fixed cost (AFC), average total cost (ATC), total revenue (TR), and marginal revenue (MR) for each total physical product (TPP) point. The P(Y) value will be incorporated into the total revenue relationship. Since P(Y) is a constant at all levels of output, the demand curve for this firm (and average revenue curve) is horizontal and P(Y)=AR=MR. This firm is a price taker or a pure competitor.

Input Area:

TPP	FC	AFC	AVC	ATC	MC	P(Y)	TR	MR
0	$700	=FC/TPP		=AFC+AVC		$60	=P(Y)*TPP	
10			$60.00		$60			
20			55.00		50			
30			50.00		40			
40			45.00		30			
50			40.00		20			
60			38.33		30			
70			38.57		40			
80			41.25		60			
90			45.56		80			
100			52.00		110			
110			60.00		140			
120			72.50		210			

MR is marginal revenue. $MR=(TR_i-TR_{i-1})/(TPP_i-TPP_{i-1})$

b. Construct a line chart of the AFC, AVC, ATC, MC and MR data. Label them appropriately. Use the TPP data for the x-axis and label it quantity of output.

c. What output would this firm choose to produce and how would this output be determined?

d. Compare the output that this firm produces at a market price of $60 with that produced at a market price of $60 in assignment 26. What can be expected to happen to output when costs decrease or increase?

30. PROFIT ANALYSIS*

a. Starting with the following worksheet data (which was developed in assignment 26), add a column for the profit formula. Calculate the profit at each level of output (TPP).

Input Area:

TPP	TR	TC	MR	MC	Profit
0	$ 0	$1500			=TR-TC
10	600	2100	60	60	
20	1200	2600	60	50	
30	1800	3000	60	40	
40	2400	3300	60	30	
50	3000	3500	60	20	

60	3600	3800	60	30
70	4200	4200	60	40
80	4800	4800	60	60
90	5400	5600	60	80
100	6000	6700	60	110
110	6600	8100	60	140
120	7200	10200	60	210

b. What is the maximum profit? What does that mean? How much output would this firm produce seeking to maximize its profit or minimize its losses? How was this quantity determined?

c. Construct two line charts: (1) a chart for the TR, TC, and profit data; plus (2) a chart for the MR and MC data. Label the data accordingly. Use the output data (TPP) for the x-axis on both charts and label it quantity of output.

d. Explain how these charts show the same optimum (profit maximizing or loss minimizing) output level.

e. WHAT IF the market price for good Y increases to $80. Put this data into the worksheet and determine the firm's optimum output and profit or loss.

31. PROFIT ANALYSIS

a. Using the following data (which was developed in assignment 25), add a column for the profit formula. Calculate the profit at each level of output (TPP).

Input Area:

TPP	TR	TC	MR	MC	Profit
0	$ 0	$1500			=TR-TC
10	500	2100	50	60	
20	1000	2600	50	50	
30	1500	3000	50	40	
40	2000	3300	50	30	
50	2500	3500	50	20	
60	3000	3800	50	30	
70	3500	4200	50	40	
80	4000	4800	50	60	
90	4500	5600	50	80	
100	5000	6700	50	110	
110	5500	8100	50	140	
120	6000	10200	50	210	

b. What is the maximum profit? How much output would this firm produce seeking to maximize its profit or minimize its losses? How was this quantity determined?

c.	Construct two line charts: (1) a chart for the TR, TC, and profit data; plus (2) a chart for the MR and MC data. Label the data accordingly. Use the output data (TPP) for the x-axis on both charts and label it quantity of output.

d.	Explain how these charts show the same optimum (profit maximizing or loss minimizing) output level.

e.	WHAT IF the market price for good Y rose to $70. Put this data into the worksheet and determine the firm's optimum output and profit or loss.

**32.	PROFIT ANALYSIS**

a.	Starting with the following worksheet data (which was developed in assignment 25), add a column for the profit formula. Calculate the profit at each level of output (TPP).
Input Area:

TPP	TR	TC	MR	MC	Profit
0	$ 0	$1500			=TR-TC
10	400	2100	40	60	
20	800	2600	40	50	
30	1200	3000	40	40	
40	1600	3300	40	30	
50	2000	3500	40	20	
60	2400	3800	40	30	
70	2800	4200	40	40	
80	3200	4800	40	60	
90	3600	5600	40	80	
100	4000	6700	40	110	
110	4400	8100	40	140	
120	4800	10200	40	210	

b.	What is the maximum profit? What does that mean? How much output would this firm produce seeking to maximize its profit or minimize its losses? How was this quantity determined?

c.	Construct two line charts: (1) a chart for the TR, TC, and profit data; plus (2) a chart for the MR and MC data. Label the data accordingly. Use the output data (TPP) for the x-axis on both charts and label it quantity of output.

d.	Explain how these charts show the same optimum (profit maximizing or loss minimizing) output level.

e.	WHAT IF the market price for good Y fell to $30. Put this data into the worksheet and determine the firm's optimum output and profit or loss.

33.   PROFIT ANALYSIS

a.   Starting with the following worksheet data (which was developed in assignment 29), add a column for the profit formula. Calculate the profit at each level of output (TPP).

Input Area:

TPP	TR	TC	MR	MC	Profit
0	$0	$700			=TR-TC
10	$600	$1,300	$60	$60	
20	$1,200	$1,800	$60	$50	
30	$1,800	$2,200	$60	$40	
40	$2,400	$2,500	$60	$30	
50	$3,000	$2,700	$60	$20	
60	$3,600	$3,000	$60	$30	
70	$4,200	$3,400	$60	$40	
80	$4,800	$4,000	$60	$60	
90	$5,400	$4,800	$60	$80	
100	$6,000	$5,900	$60	$110	
110	$6,600	$7,300	$60	$140	
120	$7,200	$9,400	$60	$210	

b.   What is the maximum profit? How much output would this firm produce seeking to maximize its profit or minimize its losses? How was this quantity determined?

c.   Construct two line charts: (1) a chart for the TR, TC, and profit data; plus (2) a chart for the MR and MC data. Label the data accordingly. Use the output data (TPP) for the x-axis and label it quantity of output.

d.   Explain how these charts show the same optimum (profit maximizing or loss minimizing) output level.

e.   WHAT IF the market price for good Y falls to $50. Put this data into the worksheet and determine the firm's optimum output and profit or loss.

34.   PROFIT ANALYSIS

a.   Starting with the following worksheet data (which was developed in assignment 29), add a column for the profit formula. Marginal revenue has been changed to $70. Calculate the profit at each level of output (TPP).

Input Area:

TPP	TR	TC	MR	MC	Profit
0	$0	$700			=TR-TC
10	$700	$1,300	$70	$60	
20	$1,400	$1,800	$70	$50	

30	$2,100	$2,200	$70	$40
40	$2,800	$2,500	$70	$30
50	$3,500	$2,700	$70	$20
60	$4,200	$3,100	$70	$30
70	$4,900	$3,400	$70	$40
80	$5,600	$4,000	$70	$60
90	$6,300	$4,800	$70	$80
100	$7,000	$5,900	$70	$110
110	$7,700	$7,300	$70	$140
120	$8,400	$9,400	$70	$210

b.   What is the maximum profit? How much output would this firm produce seeking to maximize its profit or minimize its losses? How was this quantity determined?

c.   Construct two line charts: (1) a chart for the TR, TC, and profit data; plus (2) a chart for the MR and MC data. Label the data accordingly. Use the output data (TPP) for the x-axis for both charts and label it quantity of output.

d.   Explain how these charts show the same optimum (profit maximizing or loss minimizing) output level.

e.   WHAT IF the market price for good Y increases to $80. Put this data into the worksheet and determine the firm's optimum output and profit or loss.

35.   SHORT RUN SUPPLY FOR THE PERFECT COMPETITOR*

The perfectly competitive firm is a price taker. The firm must accept the market price; any increase or reduction in its output will have no effect on the price of its product. If it raises its price, it sells nothing. If it lowers its price, it can sell no more than if it charges the market price. This results in a marginal revenue and average revenue (demand curve) for the individual firm that is horizontal and equal to the market price. Using marginal analysis, we know that any firm seeks to produce an output level where marginal revenue is equal to marginal costs. This output level also defines the supply of the perfect competitor because its average revenue or price is the same as its marginal revenue. Thus, the output point where MR=MC is also the point where output (supply) is determined by the existing market price.

a.   Construct a worksheet using the following data. Note: this data originated in assignment 25. The market price of the good (P(Y)) is provided for from possible market prices of this good in order to demonstrate the effect on output for the perfectly competitive firm. Calculate the marginal revenue (MR) for the firm for each of the possible market prices. Label the marginal revenues M_1, M_2, M_3, and M_4.

Input Area:

TPP	AVC	ATC	MC	P(Y)	MR (or AR)
0				$30	=P(Y)
10	$60.00	$210.00	$60	$40	
20	55.00	130.00	50	$60	
30	50.00	100.00	40	$80	
40	45.00	82.50	30		
50	40.00	70.00	20		
60	38.33	63.33	30		
70	38.57	60.00	40		
80	41.25	60.00	60		
90	45.56	62.22	80		
100	52.00	67.00	110		
110	60.00	73.64	140		
120	72.50	85.00	210		

b. Construct a line chart showing average variable cost, average total cost, marginal cost, and marginal revenue at each of the specified market prices. Use the output data as the x-axis.

c. A firm will seek to maximize its profit (or minimize its loss) by producing output where marginal revenue is equal to marginal cost (MR=MC). If marginal revenue is $30, what output will the firm produce?

d. What part of the perfectly competitive firm's marginal cost curve represents its short run supply curve?

36. CONSUMER AND PRODUCER SURPLUS

a. Construct a worksheet using the data provided below. Calculate the prices for each of the quantity (Q) points for demand (P(Qd)) and supply (P(Qs)). The column for quantity should range in value from 0 to 175 in increments of 25.
Input Area:

Q	P(Qd)	P(Qs)
0	=275-((5/3)*Qd)	=50.25+1.33*Qs
25		
175		

b. Construct a line chart using the data for P(Qd) and P(Qs) and label them D and S, respectively. Use the quantity (Q) data for the x-axis.

c. What is the market equilibrium price and quantity? How much would the consumer who purchased the 25th unit be willing to pay for it? Since that consumer only paid the market price, how much consumer surplus was realized when this unit sold? How much consumer surplus was realized when the 50th unit sold? How much consumer surplus was realized when the 75th unit sold?

d.   What was the minimum price the seller of the 25th unit would have been willing to take? How much producer surplus did this seller receive when the unit sold at the market price? How much producer surplus was realized when the 50th unit sold? How much producer surplus was there for the 75th unit?

37.   IMPACT OF A TAX

a.   Use the data below to prepare a worksheet that will assist in analyzing the impact (incidence) of a $4 per unit tax. The column for quantity should range in value from 0 to 20 in increments of 2. Note: P(Qs)+T is the after-tax supply equation.
Input Area:

Q (either Qd or Qs)	P(Qd)	P(Qs)	P(Qs)+T	T
0	=30-Qd	=Qs	=4+Qs	$4
2				
|				
20				

b.   Prepare a line chart showing the demand curve (P(QD)), the supply curve before tax (P(QS)), and the supply curve after tax (P(QS) + T). Use Q as the x-axis. Refer to the charting hint in assignment 19 if needed.

c.   Referring to the chart, what is the equilibrium quantity after tax? What part of the $4 tax does the buyer pay? What part of the tax does the seller pay? What is the effect of the tax on equilibrium quantity?

38.   IMPACT OF PRICE ELASTICITY ON TAX BURDEN

The relative price elasticity of supply and demand determines the relative share of the decrease in total welfare that is borne in the decrease in consumer and producer surplus. The more price elastic the demand is relative to the supply price elasticity, the larger the proportion of the welfare loss will be in reduced producer surplus. Likewise, the more price elastic the supply relative to that of demand, the larger the proportion of the welfare burden will be seen in reduced consumer surplus. Consumer surplus and producer surplus was demonstrated using market supply and demand in assignment 36.

a.   Using the data provided, construct a worksheet to show the relationship between relative price elasticity of supply and demand and the welfare burden (reduction of consumer and producer surplus) from a tax. Quantity should range from 0 to 70 in increments of 10.

Input Area:

Q	P(Qd)	P(Qs)	P(Qs)+T	T	PE(D)	PE(S)
0	=150-2*Qd	=Qs	=30+Qs	$30	=P/(P-VID)	=P/(P-VIS)
10						
|						
70						

Q represents the quantity of the good and can be either Qd or Qs.

P(Qd) is the demand relationship expressed as price being a function of quantity.

P(Qs) is the supply relationship expressed as price being a function of quantity.

P(Qs)+T represents the supply relationship after the tax.

T represents the tax.

PE(D) represents the price elasticity of demand. PE(D)=P/(P-VID) where VID is the vertical intercept of the demand curve.

PE(S) represents the price elasticity of supply. PE(S)=P/(P-VIS) where VIS is the vertical intercept of the supply curve.

Note: These elasticity relationships were demonstrated in assignments 8 and 14.

Calculate the price data for each quantity (Q) point using the demand relationship (P(Qd)), the supply relationship (P(Qs)), and the supply relationship after the tax (P(Qs)+T). Also calculate the price elasticity of demand at each quantity point, for supply and for supply after the tax. The vertical intercepts are readily determined by examining the price and quantity data calculated.

b.   Construct a line chart of the price data from the demand (P(Qd)), the supply (P(Qs)), and the supply after the tax (P(Qs)+T). Label these D, S, and S+T respectively. Use the quantity (Q) data for the x-axis.

c.   What is the equilibrium price and quantity before the tax? What is the equilibrium price and quantity after the tax is imposed? What has happened to total welfare as a result of the tax?

d.   Which has decreased by the greater amount, consumer or producer surplus? Which is more price elastic, demand or supply? Explain using the data calculated. How much tax revenue is the government collecting from its tax on this good?

39.   IMPACT OF PRICE ELASTICITY ON TAX BURDEN

The relative price elasticity of supply and demand determines the relative share of the decrease in total welfare that is borne in the decrease in consumer and producer surplus. The more price elastic the demand is relative to the supply price elasticity, the larger the proportion of the welfare loss will be in reduced producer surplus. Likewise, the more price elastic the supply relative to that of demand, the larger the proportion of the welfare burden will be seen in reduced consumer surplus. Consumer surplus and producer surplus was demonstrated using market supply and demand in assignment 36.

a.   Using the data provided below, construct a worksheet to show the relationship between relative price elasticity of supply and demand and the welfare burden (reduction of consumer and producer surplus) from a tax. Quantity should range from 0 to 90 in increments of 10.

Input Area:

Q	P(Qd)	P(Qs)	P(Qs)+T	T	PE(D)	PE(S)
0	=120-.5*Qd	=Qs	=15+Qs	$15	=P/(P-VID)	=P/(P-VIS)
10						
|						
90						

Q represents the quantity of the good and can be either Qd or Qs.
P(Qd) is the demand relationship expressed as price being a function of quantity.
P(Qs) is the supply relationship expressed as price being a function of quantity.
P(Qs)+T represents the supply relationship after the tax.
T represents the tax.
PE(D) represents the price elasticity of demand. PE(D)=P/(P-VID) where VID is the vertical intercept of the demand curve.
PE(S) represents the price elasticity of supply. PE(S)=P/(P-VIS) where VIS is the vertical intercept of the supply curve.
Note: These elasticity relationships were demonstrated in assignments 8 and 14.

Calculate the price data for each quantity (Q) point using the demand relationship (P(Qd)), the supply relationship (P(Qs)), and the supply relationship after the tax (P(Qs)+T). Also calculate the price elasticity of demand at each quantity point, for supply and for supply after the tax. The vertical intercepts are readily determined by examining the price and quantity data calculated.

b.   Construct a line chart of the price data from the demand (P(Qd)), the supply (P(Qs)), and the supply after the tax (P(Qs)+T). Label these D, S, and S+T respectively. Use the quantity (Q) data for the x-axis.

c.   What is the equilibrium price and quantity before the tax? What is the equilibrium price and quantity after the tax is imposed? What has happened to total welfare as a result of the tax?

d.   Which has decreased by the greater amount, consumer or producer surplus? Which is more price elastic, demand or supply? Explain using the data calculated. How much tax revenue will the government receive from this tax?

40.   EFFECT OF MINIMUM WAGE ON THE MARKET FOR LABOR

a.   Using the data provided below, construct a worksheet to display the market for unskilled labor. The values for quantity should range from 0 to 19 in increments of 1. Calculate the wage at each quantity point based on the demand for unskilled labor (P(Qd)). Calculate the wage at each quantity point based on the supply of unskilled labor (P(Qs)). Calculate the minimum wage at each quantity point.
Input Area:

Q (Qd or Qs)	P(Qd)	P(Qs)	min. wage
0	= 12-.7*Qd	= -2+.7Qs	$6.40
1			
|			
19			

Q represents quantity of labor in millions.
P(Qd) is the demand for unskilled labor expressed as price of labor (wage) being a
   function of the quantity. Recall that the demand for labor is derived
   demand and is directly related to the marginal value product (MVP) of this
   type of labor. The MVP is the value of the output that this type of labor
   can produce.
P(Qs) is the supply of unskilled labor expressed as the price of labor (wage) being
   a function of the quantity of labor. Recall that the supply of any good,
   service, or factor (input) is based on its opportunity cost or next best
   alternative.
Minimum wage is a price floor below which it is illegal to exchange labor
   services.

b.   Construct a line chart for labor demand (P(Qd)), labor supply (P(Qs)), and the minimum wage. Label them D, S, and min. wage respectively. Use the quantity (Q) data for the x-axis.

c.   What is the market equilibrium wage and quantity? With a minimum wage price floor of $6.40, what is the quantity of unskilled labor demanded? What is the quantity of unskilled labor supplied?

d.   What do we call the situation when a market price results in the quantity supplied being greater than the quantity demanded? The minimum wage has resulted in a long run situation where quantity supplied is greater than quantity demanded by how much? What would normally happen in the absence of the minimum wage when such a surplus existed? How do we classify those who want to work at the market wage but cannot find a job? How many unskilled will actually be working?

41.   IMPACT OF A PRICE CEILING

a.   Using the data provided below, construct a worksheet to show the market for efficiency apartments in a large city that has imposed rent control (a price ceiling on rent to keep apartments "reasonably" priced). For each quantity point: calculate the price based on the demand for apartments (PQd)), the price based on the supply for apartments (P(Qs)), and the rent control maximum ceiling (ceiling).
Input Area:

Q (Qd or Qs)	P(Qd)	P(Qs)	ceiling
0	=1400-(10*Qd)	=200+(10*Qs)	$600
20			
40			
60			
80			
100			
120			

b.   Construct a line chart for the demand price data (P(Qd)), the supply price data (P(Qs)), and the rent control ceiling (ceiling). Label them D, S, and ceiling respectively. Use the quantity data (Q) for the x-axis.

c.   In the absence of rent control, what would be the equilibrium rent and number of apartments being occupied? With the rent control price ceiling, how many units are being rented? How many people are willing and able to rent at the rent control price? What long run situation has the rent control price ceiling caused?

d.   Considering the number of units actually being rented at the rent control price ceiling, what has happened to the <u>total</u> of consumer surplus and producer surplus in this market?

42.   ECONOMIES OF SCALE

It is not uncommon for the production of goods and services to have economies of scale (falling long run average cost) due to efficiencies in size. This means the average costs decrease as the size or scale increases. It is not true that all production shows significant economies of scale or those that do continue to show lower costs as scale continues to increase. Constant returns (constant average cost) and decreasing returns to scale (increasing average cost) are to be expected as size increases costs when management inefficiencies or other inefficiencies result from becoming increasingly large. If production to satisfy total market demand occurs where economies of scale are still operative or where constant returns to scale are at a level that can satisfy market demand with only one or a very few firms, the market structure will be naturally limited. This is called a natural barrier to entry. The extreme case would result in a natural monopoly.

a.   Using the data below, construct a worksheet which demonstrates a typical long run average cost curve for a production process that shows economies of scale, constant returns and diseconomies of scale, and a market demand curve that would result in natural barriers to entry. Calculate the price data for each quantity (Q) point using the demand relationship (P(Qd)).

Input Area:

Q	LRATC	P(Qd)
0	$120	=220-2*Q
10	$107	
20	$95	
30	$85	
40	$76	
50	$69	
60	$63	
70	$60	
80	$60	
90	$60	
100	$60	
110	$60	
120	$61	
130	$64	
140	$68	
150	$75	
160	$83	
170	$94	
180	$109	

Q represents the quantity of the good in thousands.

LRATC represents the long run average cost of a firm.

P(Qd) represents the market demand relationship expressed as price being a function of quantity.

b.   Construct a line chart for the LRATC and P(Qd) data. Label them LRATC and D, respectively. Use the quantity (Q) data for the x-axis.

c.   Over what range of output does this firm experience: (1) economies of scale, (2) constant returns, and (3) diseconomies of scale?

d.   Given the total market demand, how many firms would naturally result in this market? Why?

e.   Suppose the market demand were multiple (say 5 to 10) times larger than shown. What size firms would likely result? About how many firms would likely occupy this market?

43.   MONOPOLIST UNIT REVENUE

Since the monopolist firm is the only supplier in its market, the market demand is also the demand for the firm. The monopolist is a price searcher in that changes in its output produced will cause the market equilibrium price to change. Since the monopolist firm will sell all of its output at the highest price the market demand will allow, the market demand curve is also the firm's average revenue curve. Since the average revenue is falling as the firm increases its output, its marginal revenue must also be falling and lie below the average revenue. Marginal revenue can be calculated using the basic definitions for total revenue (PQ) and marginal revenue (change in total revenue/change in quantity).

a.   Construct a worksheet using the data provided below to show the average and marginal revenue of a monopolist firm (or other type of price searching firm). The values for quantity (Q) should range from 0 to 130 in increments of 10. Calculate the values for TR, AR, and MR for each applicable quantity data point.

Input Area:

Q	P(Qd)	TR	AR	MR
0	$=55-.5*Qd$	$=P*Q$ or $P(Qd)*Q$	$=TR/Q$ or $P(Qd)$	$=(TR_i-Tr_{i-1})/(Q_i-Q_{i-1})$
10				
$\mid$				
130				

P(Qd) is price as a function of quantity demanded.
TR represents total revenue.
AR represents average revenue.
MR represents marginal revenue.

b.   Construct a line chart for average revenue (AR) and marginal revenue (MR) data. Label them D=AR and MR, respectively. Use the quantity data for the x-axis.

c.   When the marginal revenue becomes negative, what does this imply about total revenue? Why would a firm never choose to produce an output quantity where marginal revenue was negative?

d.   Why does a firm always produce where its demand is elastic (i.e., greater than 1)?

44. MONOPOLIST PROFIT*

a. Using the data provided below (which comes from assignment 25), construct a worksheet to show both the unit costs and revenue for a monopolist (or other price searcher) firm in order to determine its optimum output and profit. The values for quantity should range from 0 to 120 in increments of 10. For each level of output (Q), calculate values for: total revenue (TR), average revenue (AR), marginal revenue (MR), and profit.

Input Area:

Q	AVC	ATC	MC	TR	AR	MR	Profit
0							
10	$60.00	$210.00	$60				
20	55.00	130.00	50				
30	50.00	100.00	40				
40	45.00	82.50	30				
50	40.00	70.00	20				
60	38.33	63.33	30				
70	38.57	60.00	40				
80	41.25	60.00	60				
90	45.56	62.22	80				
100	52.00	67.00	110				
110	60.00	73.64	140				
120	72.50	85.00	210				

Note: Using the definitions and formulas developed in assignment 43, relationships for total revenue (TR), average revenue (AR), and marginal revenue (MR) were added.

$TR=PQ$ or $TR=AR*Q$

$AR=118-.8*Q$

$MR=(TR_i-TR_{i-1})/(Q_i-Q_{i-1})$

$Profit=(AR-ATC)*Q$ or $Profit=TR-TC$

Since $TR=PQ$ or $AR*Q$ and $TC=ATC*Q$, the following formula can be used to find the profit at each level of output: $Profit=(AR-ATC)*Q$.

b. Using marginal analysis, what rule and level of output would this firm choose to produce in order to maximize its profit (or minimize its short run losses)?

c. Construct a line chart for the unit cost data (AVC, ATC, and MC) and the unit revenue data (AR and MR). Use the quantity data for the x-axis.

d. Using the chart, determine the level of output the firm should produce in order to maximize its profit, and the price it could sell the good for. Explain how you used the chart to determine these values.

e. Is the firm making a profit or loss? Explain your answer by using the chart. Using the data for profit that was calculated, determine how much profit this firm will be making. What would happen to the optimum output and profit if the market demand curve shifted to the left?

45. IMPACT OF SUBSIDY ON PROFIT

Governments, for a variety of political reasons, sometimes decide to subsidize a producer to encourage production of a good or service. By using unit cost and revenue analysis, we can demonstrate the impact of a subsidy and compare the cost in government revenue spent versus the results. Note: The values for quantity (Q), average total cost (ATC), marginal cost (MC), average cost (AR), and marginal revenue (MR) are taken from assignment 44.

a. Using the data below, construct a worksheet to demonstrate the unit cost and revenue data before and after a government subsidy. Calculate the profit at each level of output (Q) before the subsidy (Profit) and after the subsidy is implemented (Profit w/S).

Input Area:

Q	ATC	MC	S	ATC-S	MC-S	AR	MR	Profit
0			$26	=ATC-S	=MC-S			=(AR-ATC)*Q
10	$210.00	$60		$184.00	$34	$110	$110	or
20	130.00	50		104.00	24	102	94	=TR-TC
30	100.00	40		74.00	14	94	78	
40	82.50	30		56.50	4	86	62	
50	70.00	20		44.00	-6	78	46	
60	63.33	30		37.33	4	70	30	
70	60.00	40		34.00	14	62	14	
80	60.00	60		34.00	34	54	-2	
90	62.22	80		36.22	54	46	-18	
100	67.00	110		41.00	84	38	-34	
110	73.64	140		47.64	114	30	-50	
120	85.00	210		59.00	184	22	-66	

S represents the subsidy per unit of output.
ATC-S and MC-S represent the unit cost curves after the subsidy is implemented.

b. By how much did the subsidy increase the firm's maximum profit?

c. Construct a line chart using the data for the unit cost curves before the subsidy (ATC and MC), after the subsidy (ATC-S and MC-S), and the revenue curves (AR and MR). Label them accordingly, but use D=AR for the AR data. Use the quantity (Q) data for the x-axis.

d.   What will happen to the output produced by this firm? What happens to the price at which the firm sells its output?

e.   What has happened to consumer surplus for this firm's product? What has happened to this firm's producer surplus? What is the cost to taxpayers for the subsidy?

46.   MONOPOLISTIC COMPETITION LONG RUN EQUILIBRIUM

In a market structure where there are a large number of firms producing a very similar, but differentiated product plus good market information and low barriers to entry, economic profits will not exist in long run equilibrium. For the individual firm, short run economic profits (or losses) are quite possible, but the good information and low costs of entry (or exit) will result in the typical monopolistic competitor making zero economic profits (i.e., normal profit which is included as an implicit opportunity cost in the average total costs of the firm). The key to understanding this long run equilibrium in the market is to recognize the impact which the entry or exit of competitors has on the individual firm's average revenue (or individual demand) and marginal revenue. With the entry of more competitors, the individual firm's demand decreases (shifts to the left) and becomes more price elastic. When competitors exit the market (due to losses), the firm's demand curve increases (shifts to the right) and becomes less price elastic.

a.   Using the data provided below, construct a worksheet in order to demonstrate the effects on a typical monopolistic competitor when economic profits provide incentive for the entry of additional competitors into its market. Calculate the firm's profit (or loss) at each quantity point using its cost data and its original revenue data. Label this data as Profit. Calculate the firm's profit (or loss) at each quantity point using its cost data and its new revenue data. Label this data as Profit'.

Input Area:

Q	ATC	MC	AR	MR	AR'	MR'	Profit
0			$148.50		$117.82		
5	$270.00	$150.00	$144.00	$144	$114.00	$114.00	
10	$210.00	$105.00	$139.50	$135	$110.18	$106.37	
15	$175.00	$80.00	$135.00	$126	$106.37	$98.73	
20	$151.25	$60.00	$130.50	$117	$102.55	$91.09	
25	$133.00	$45.00	$126.00	$108	$98.73	$83.46	
30	$118.33	$35.00	$121.50	$99	$94.91	$75.82	
35	$106.43	$27.00	$117.00	$90	$91.09	$68.18	
40	$96.50	$22.00	$112.50	$81	$87.28	$60.55	
45	$88.22	$20.00	$108.00	$72	$83.46	$52.91	
50	$81.40	$22.00	$103.50	$63	$79.64	$45.28	
55	$76.00	$25.50	$99.00	$54	$75.82	$37.64	
60	$72.00	$30.00	$94.50	$45	$72.00	$30.00	

65	$68.58	$36.00	$90.00	$36	$68.18	$22.37
70	$66.25	$46.00	$85.50	$27	$64.37	$14.73
75	$64.90	$60.00	$81.00	$18	$60.55	$7.10
80	$64.59	$80.00	$76.50	$9	$56.73	-$0.54
85	$65.50	$103.00	$72.00	$0	$52.91	-$8.18
90	$67.58	$130.00	$67.50	-$9	$49.09	-$15.81
95	$70.87	$165.00	$63.00	-$18	$45.28	-$23.45
100	$75.58	$210.00	$58.50	-$27	$41.46	-$31.09
105	$81.98	$270.00	$54.00	-$36	$37.64	-$38.72
110	$90.53	$380.00	$49.50	-$45	$33.82	-$46.36

> Note: The following relationships for the firm's original average revenue and marginal revenue are listed only for informational purposes. Assignments 25 and 43 required calculation of the data using such relationships including the unit cost relationships.
>
> $AR = 148.5 - .9*Q$
>
> $MR = ((AR_i*Q_i) - (AR_{i-1}*Q_{i-1}))/(Q_i - Q_{i-1})$
>
> $AR' = 117.82 - .76362*Q$ This represents the change in the firm's average revenue with the associated marginal revenue as MR'.
>
> Profit $= (AR - ATC)*Q$ (this is equivalent to Profit $= TR - TC$)

b. Construct a line chart for the unit cost data (ATC and MC), the firm's original revenue data (AR=D and MR), and its new revenue data (AR'=D' and MR'). Label them appropriately as indicated. Use the quantity (Q) data as the x-axis.

c. What is the firm's profit maximizing output, market price, and profit with the original revenue? How was the profit maximizing output determined using the firm's cost and revenue data?

d. After the revenue changed (AR' and MR'), what are the firm's profit maximizing quantity, price, and profit? As new entry occurs, what is noticeable about the output, market price of the product, and profits of this firm? Why is it reasonable to expect the long run equilibrium of the typical monopolistic competitor to be at zero economic profits?

47.   PERFECT COMPETITOR'S MARGINAL REVENUE PRODUCT

Note: The data for the quantity of the variable factor (Q(B)), output of product Y (TPP), and the definition for marginal physical product (MPP) are taken from assignment 23. Since this firm is a perfect competitor, it has a constant market price (average revenue) at all levels of its output (P(Y)). Marginal revenue (MR) is also equal to the market price at all levels of output. The marginal revenue product (MRP) for a unit of the variable factor is the marginal revenue added to the firm's total revenue that the additional quantity of the factor produced. This is calculated by multiplying the marginal physical product

(MPP) produced by adding that unit of the factor, by the additional revenue (MR) the MPP units of output brought to the firm when sold. The MRP represents the value to the firm of the additional unit(s) of the factor.

a.   Using the data provided below, construct a worksheet to show the relationships between the marginal physical product (MPP) of a variable factor or input (usually labor) and the marginal revenue product (MRP) for that same factor under the conditions of perfect competition. Calculate the MPP and the MRP for each separate operating level of the variable factor (Q(B)).

Input Area:

Q(B)	TPP	MPP		P(Y)	MRP
0	0	$=(TPP_i-TPP_{i-1})/(Q(B)_i-Q(B)_{i-1})$		$10	=MR*MPP
5	5			=MR	
10	11				
15	20				
20	33.5				
25	49				
30	63				
35	73				
40	80				
45	85				
50	88				
55	90				
60	91				
65	90				

b.   Construct separate line charts for the MPP and MRP data. Use the quantity of the variable factor (Q(B)) data for the x-axis.

c.   Why would a firm never choose to produce using less than 25 units of the variable factor?

d.   WHAT IF each unit of the variable factor cost the firm $20, how many units of this factor would the firm choose to purchase based on its MRP? Why?

48.   MONOPOLIST'S MARGINAL REVENUE PRODUCT

Note: The data for the quantity of the variable factor (Q(B)), output of product Y (TPP), and the definition for marginal physical product (MPP) are taken from assignment 22. The definition of marginal revenue product (MRP) is taken from assignment 47. Because this firm is a monopolist, its average revenue is the market demand. As the firm increases output (TPP), its price or the average revenue (AR) of its product Y will fall. As shown in assignment 42, the marginal revenue (MR) will be less than its average revenue.

a. Using the data provided below, construct a worksheet to show the relationships between the marginal physical product (MPP) of a variable factor or input (usually labor) and the marginal revenue product (MRP) for that same factor under conditions of monopoly. Calculate the marginal physical product (MPP) and marginal revenue product (MRP) for each quantity level of the variable factor (Q(B)).

Input Area:

Q(B)	TPP	MPP	AR	MR	MRP
0	0	$=(TPP_i-TPP_{i-1})/(Q(B)_i-Q(B)_{i-1})$			$=MR*MPP$
5	5		$52.50	$55	
10	11		$50.00	$50	
15	20		$47.50	$45	
20	33.5		$45.00	$40	
25	49		$42.50	$35	
30	63		$40.00	$30	
35	73		$37.50	$25	
40	80		$35.00	$20	
45	85		$32.50	$15	
50	88		$30.00	$10	
55	90		$27.50	$5	
60	91		$25.00	$0	
65	90		$22.50	-$5	

b. Construct separate line charts for the marginal physical product (MPP) and marginal revenue product (MRP) data. Use the quantity of the variable factor (Q(B)) data for the x-axis.

c. Why does the MRP for the monopolist decline at a faster rate than the MPP?

d. What part of the MRP curve represents the demand of the firm for the variable factor B? Explain.

49. LABOR DEMAND AND SUPPLY

The labor market is a factor (or resource or input) market. As such, the demand for labor is a derived demand based on the value of the goods and services that labor can produce. The marginal revenue product (MRP) measures the value of the marginal product in terms of what this output adds to the firm's total revenue. Given diminishing returns to a variable factor (in this case labor) in the short run, the MRP declines as the variable factor is added to a fixed plant and capital stock. The demand for labor in the labor market is the summation of the individual firm's demand for labor based on labor's MRP. The demand for labor will be positively correlated with any variable that affects the MRP of labor.

The supply of labor is determined by the willingness and ability of workers to offer their labor services. As with all supplies of factors, this represents the opportunity costs of the factor (in this case, workers). Such alternate opportunities as education, leisure, self-employment, welfare, or charitable assistance represent some of the factors that influence this willingness and ability to offer labor services. The wage represents the benefit of offering labor services, as well as the cost to the employer of buying these services. The higher the wage, the more labor services will be offered both by new entrants as well as current labor suppliers increasing their supply of labor (working more hours). The income derived from labor represents by far the largest source of income to households in developed countries.

a. Using the data provided below, construct a worksheet to represent the labor market supply and demand for labor. At each quantity (Q) point, calculate the price data based on the demand for labor (P(Qd)) and the price data based on the supply for labor (P(Qs)). The values for Q should range from 0 to 190 in increments of 10.
    Input Area:

Q (Qd or Qs)	P(Qd)	P(Qs)
0	=113-.7*Qd	= -30+.4*Qs
10		
|		
190		

Q represents the quantity of labor in millions.
Note that the demand for labor resembles the usual inverse relationship between price (wage) and quantity demanded for any good based on the falling marginal revenue product of labor in the short run. The supply of labor resembles the usual positive relationship between price (wage) and quantity supplied for any good based on a higher wage attracting labor services from other opportunities or alternative pursuits.

b. Construct a line chart of the data for price based on demand (P(Qd)) and the data for price based on supply (P(Qs)). Label them DL and SL, respectively. Use the quantity (Q) data for the x-axis.

c. What is the equilibrium wage and quantity employed in the labor market at this demand and supply for labor? Are there more people who wish to work?

d. Suppose there was a major technological breakthrough accompanied by the implementation of this technology in the workplace (increased physical capital and human capital) so that the productivity of labor increased (marginal physical product increased at every quantity of labor employed). What would happen in the labor market and what would happen to the equilibrium wage and employment?

e.   Suppose work requirements were instituted for receiving welfare payments and educational assistance, making these less attractive alternatives to work. What would happen in the labor market and what would be the result in the equilibrium wage and quantity of labor employed?

50.   MONOPSONY

Monopsony is a factor market condition where there is only one buyer of a resource, such as labor in an isolated community. In the case of a competitive resource market where the demand of one firm has a negligible effect on total market demand and, therefore, the market price, the market price is also the marginal cost (MC) of that resource over the range of its use of this resource. The firm considers the supply of the resource to be constant at the resource market price. Its average cost and marginal cost are identical. The firm's demand for a resource is that resource's marginal revenue product (MRP). The firm will purchase all units so long as the MRP is greater than or equal to its MC. In such a case, it chooses to buy all units of the resource up to the point where the MRP is equal to the market price of the resource.

When there is only one buyer of the resource, the firm buys more of the resource and the market price for the resource increases in accordance with the market supply of labor. This means that the market price of the resource is not constant and the marginal cost of buying more of the resource rises above the market price. The result is that a monopsonist firm will not choose to buy all units of the resource until MRP is equal to the price of the resource, but will only purchase units until MRP is equal to the MC of the resource.

a.   Using the following data, construct a worksheet in order to show the effect of monopsony on a resource market. Calculate the price data at each quantity (Q_L) point using the market supply relationship (P(Qs) or S_L). Also calculate the marginal cost of labor to the firm (MC_L) for each quantity point. Values for Q_L should range from 0 to 65 in increments of 5.

Input Area:

Q_L	MRP_L or D_L	P(Qs) or S_L	MC_L
0		=-4.5+.4333*Q	=$((P(Qs)_i * Q_i)-(P(Qs)_{i-1} * Q_{i-1}))/(Q_i - Q_{i-1})$ or
5			=$(TC_i - TC_{i-1})/(Q_i - Q_{i-1})$
10			
15			
20			
25	$108.50		
30	$84.00		
35	$50.00		
40	$28.00		
45	$15.00		
50	$6.00		

55	$2.00
60	$0.00
65	

P(Qs) or S_L represents the market supply of labor.

MC_L represents the marginal cost of labor and is calculated from the basic definition of marginal cost: the change in total cost of labor divided by the change in labor employed. Since the total of a given quantity of labor is the market price multiplied by the number of units, the P(Qs) data can represent the market price at each quantity of labor employed.

Q_L and MRP_L data are taken from assignment 47.

b. Construct a line chart of the data for MRP_L, P(Qs), and MC_L. Label them DL, SL, and MCL, respectively. Use the quantity (QL) data for the x-axis.

c. Given marginal decision making by this monopsonist firm, how many units of labor will it choose to employ? Using the market supply (S_L), what will the market wage rate be?

d. Supposing the D_L curve represented the summation of many firms' marginal revenue product for labor demand, what would the equilibrium wage and quantity be? What can be concluded about the effects of monopsony on resource price and use?

51. PRESENT VALUE*

A dollar today has more value than a dollar in the future, even if there is no inflation. The reason for this is that we have the opportunity to take a present-day dollar and save it while earning interest. In the future, our present dollar will have grown by the compounded interest payments earned. This is the basic principle upon which the present value of any future payment is calculated. The present value represents how much money must be kept in savings in order to equal the future payment (or future value) at the prevailing interest rate. When the interest rate is used in this manner, it may be referred to as a discount rate, because one is discounting future values by the opportunity to grow a present value at a set rate of return (in this case, the interest rate). The formula or relationship that equates a present value (PV) to a future value (FV) is: $PV = FV/(1+r)^n$

or $PV = FV/(1+r)\wedge n$ (for worksheet calculation)

"r" represents the interest or discount rate expressed in decimal form.

"n" represents the number of interest periods until the future value is due. If an annual interest rate is being used, then "n" represents the number of years. If it is a monthly interest rate, then "n" would be the number of months.

a. Using the following data, construct a worksheet to calculate the present value (PV) of four future payments (FV). Label the present values PV_1, PV_2, PV_3, and PV_4.

Input Area:

FV	r	n	PV
$1,000.00	0.05	1	=FV/(1+r)^n
$1,000.00	0.05	10	
$1,000.00	0.1	1	
$1,000.00	0.1	10	

b. Comparing PV_1 to PV_3, what is the effect on the present value of a higher discount or interest rate? Explain why this makes sense.

c. Comparing PV_2 to PV_1, what is the effect of a future payment being payable farther in the future on its present value? Explain why this makes sense.

d. Comparing PV_1 to PV_3 and PV_2 to PV_4, what happens to the difference between present values at different interest rates for a longer term compared to a shorter term until the future payment is due? What causes this effect?

52. FUTURE VALUE

A dollar has more value in the future than it has today, even if there is no inflation. In other words, the future value (FV) of a dollar today is greater than its present value (PV). This is because today's savings will grow over time based on its ability to earn compounded interest. In the future, the amount will have grown into a larger future value. This is the basic principle upon which the future value of a present sum is calculated. The calculated future value represents how much this present sum would grow if saved for a specific time in the future at a specific interest rate or rate of return. This includes the effects of compounding (earning a return on interest earned in earlier periods of the term of future saving). The present value (PV) relationship is algebraically manipulated to solve for the future value (FV): $FV=PV(1+r)^n$ [On the worksheet: FV=PV*(1+r)^n]

"r" represents the interest or discount rate expressed in decimal form.
"n" represents the number of interest periods until the future value is due. If an annual interest rate is being used, then "n" represents the number of years. If it is a monthly interest, then "n" would be the number of months.

a. Using the following data, construct a worksheet to calculate the future vale (FV) for four present sums to be held for differing interest rate and time period combinations.

Input Area:

PV	r	n	FV
$1,000.00	0.05	1	=PV*(1+r)^n
$1,000.00	0.05	10	
$1,000.00	0.1	1	
$1,000.00	0.1	10	

b.   Comparing FV_1 to FV_2, what is the effect on future value if the time period is lengthened? Why is the difference in value more than simply the interest rate times the number of interest rate payments? How much compounded interest was included in FV_2?

c.   Comparing FV_1 to FV_3, what can be concluded about the effect of a higher rate of return or interest rate on the future value of a present sum?

d.   Comparing FV_1 to FV_3 and FV_2 to FV_4, what happens to the difference between future values at different interest rates at a longer term compared to a shorter term until the future value is computed? Why does this happen?

53.   INVESTMENT DECISION

One of the most difficult decisions a firm must make is a decision on making a long-term investment in capital goods. The reason for this is two fold. There is risk involved with estimating the return (revenue) that such a long-term commitment will yield over its life. Secondly, the estimated returns from the investment are difficult to compare to the up front investment cost due to the time value of money or the difference between present and future values of sums. The use of the present value/future value relationship can be used to solve the second difficulty and assist in deciding if an investment is a good decision or not (holding relative risk out of consideration). Since there are always various options for investment funds, the concept of opportunity cost in such a decision must be considered.

a.   Using the data provided, construct a worksheet to compare the present value of the estimated future revenue of a given investment to its actual investment cost. Calculate the present value (PV) of the expected future revenue (FV_i) from this investment using interest rate r and interest rate r'.

I	FV_i	n_i	r	PV	r'
$10,000	$3500	1	0.05		0.08
	$3500	2			
	$4500	3			

$$PV = FV_1 / (1 + r)^{n1} + FV_2 / (1 + r)^{n2} + FV_3 / (1 + r)^{n3}$$ or in worksheet form:
=FV₁/(1+r)^n₁+FV₂/(1+r)^n₂+FV₃/(1+r)^n₃

The basic present value relationship is $PV=FV/(1+r)^n$ where "r" is the interest discount rate expressed as a decimal and "n" is the number of interest time periods until the future payment is received. In this case, there are three separate payments expected from the investment, to be received at the end of years 1, 2, and 3, respectively. The third payment (FV_3) is larger because it includes salvage value for the capital good.

When calculating the sum of the present values of these three expected future payments, using the discount interest rate that is plausible for other alternatives (i.e., saving at the market interest rate or other investment alternatives), one is determining the amount available for investing today in order to realize those future payments at the given interest rate. Comparing what is actually on hand to invest (I) with the present value of these expected payments, one can determine whether this is a good investment.

b. At the original interest rate (r), is the present value larger or smaller than the required investment cost (I)? At an expected interest rate or rate of return of r, is this a good investment? Explain.

c. Would this investment be a good decision at the interest/discount rate of r'? Explain.

d. What do you conclude about the importance of market interest rates on investment?

54.   PRODUCTION POSSIBILITIES FRONTIER CURVE*

A production possibilities frontier curve indicates maximum production of output combinations of two or more goods with full employment of all resources. The following table indicates a production possibilities frontier when there are only two alternative outputs: computer game software (good A) and food (good B). Each paired quantities represents possible combinations that could be produced with a given amount of resources and technology.

Input Area:

Q(A)	Q(B)
0	44,000
4,000	43,500
8,000	43,000
12,000	42,000
16,000	41,000
20,000	39,000
24,000	35,500
28,000	32,000
32,000	27,000

36,000	21,000
40,000	14,000
44,000	0

a.   Prepare a worksheet containing the quantities listed in the table. Note: Autofill can be used for good A since it increases by a uniform amount. (Autofill review: Type in the first two values of the series and highlight those cells. Put the cursor on the box in the bottom right corner of the cell, the cursor will turn to a "+." Click and drag the mouse over the cells you want to fill.)

b.   Prepare a line chart for the production possibilities frontier. Use the values for software as the x-axis.

55.   EFFECT OF TECHNOLOGY ON OUTPUT USING PRODUCTION POSSIBILITIES FRONTIER CURVE ANALYSIS

Advances in technology enable the production possibilities frontier to expand. For example, if new and better ways to grow food are developed, then farmers can produce more food using this new technology and more resources can be shifted to produce more of other goods, such as software.

a.   Using the data provided below, prepare a worksheet indicating the impact of technology on the production of food.
Input Area:

Q(A)	Q(B)	Q'(B)
0	44,000	49,000
4,000	43,500	48,500
8,000	43,000	48,000
12,000	42,000	47,000
16,000	41,000	46,000
20,000	39,000	44,000
24,000	35,500	40,500
28,000	32,000	37,000
32,000	27,000	32,000
36,000	21,000	26,000
40,000	14,000	19,000
44,000	0	5,000

Q(A) represents quantities of software.
Q(B) represents quantities of food units before technology improvement.
Q'(B) represents quantities of food units after technology improvement.

b. Prepare a line chart illustrating the impact of new technology on the production possibilities frontier. On the chart, show food units before technology and food units after technology. Use quantities of good A (Q(A)) as the x-axis.

56. MARGINAL ANALYSIS

Marginal analysis is based on the principle that an activity should be increased up to the point where the marginal benefit is equal to the marginal cost. Since almost all resources are scarce (or limited), a firm must frequently decide how to use their resources among competing beneficial alternatives. The goal is to achieve the maximum total benefit possible from a given amount of resource when dividing it between two or more alternatives. Using marginal analysis and allocating each unit according to the principle that its marginal benefit (MB) must be greater than or at least equal to its marginal cost (MC), will result in the best allocation to maximize total benefit of the resource. The concept of opportunity cost is also illustrated in such a typical situation because the opportunity cost of using one more unit of the scarce resource for one of the available alternatives is the benefit it would have produced in the next best alternative use. Marginal analysis can be illustrated using a situation with two beneficial alternatives (watching TV and studying economics) and a scarce resource (time). Both of the alternatives (TV and economics) exhibit the law of diminishing returns (or utility).

a. Using the data provided below, construct a worksheet to illustrate the use of marginal analysis by determining and comparing marginal benefit (in this case, marginal utility) and marginal cost (in this case, marginal opportunity cost) of an activity (TV) where time is limited and two beneficial alternatives exist. Calculate the marginal utility for each hour spent watching TV (MU(TV)), each hour spent studying economics (MU(econ)), and the MC(TV).

Input Area:

Q	TU(TV)	TU(econ)	MU	H	MC(TV)
0	0	0	$=(TU_i-TU_{i-1})/(Q_i-Q_{i-1})$	8 hours	$=MU(econ)_{H-i}$
1	70	80			where i is number of hours
2	100	138			committed to TV
3	115	178			of the hours available (H)
4	125	206			
5	131	226			
6	135	241			
7	137	252			
8	138	261			

Q represents the number of hours committed to an activity.

TU is the total utility (or benefit) from a given number of hours of an activity.

MU is the marginal utility (or marginal benefit) of an activity. This is the additional utility (or benefit) for an additional amount of the resource (time) used in that activity.

H represents the limit on the scarce resource (time).

The marginal cost of an activity is the benefit lost from the other activity when a unit of the resource is used for the activity rather than its alternative. In this case, the MC of TV is the marginal utility foregone when an hour is taken from studying economics (econ) and used for TV. For example, when one hour is used for TV, it leaves only seven hours for studying economics, so the marginal cost of that first hour of TV is the lost benefit from the eighth hour of studying economics. If a second hour is spent watching TV, the MU of the seventh hour studying economics is its MC, and so forth.

b. Construct a line chart for the MU(TV) and MC(TV) data. Use the number of hours (Q) for the x-axis. The y-axis is in units of utility.

c. How many hours of TV should this individual choose? How much marginal benefit would he or she receive for the last hour of TV watched? What would be the marginal cost of that last hour of TV?

d. Add the total utilities for the combinations of TV and studying time possible (8, 0, 7, 1, and so forth). How do these totals support marginal analysis? Since the marginal benefit of the last hour spent watching TV was exactly equal to the marginal cost, what does that imply about using one hour less for TV and using it for studying instead (assuming each hour must be used for only one activity)?

57. NEGATIVE EXTERNALITY

When the production, sale, or use of a good imposes costs on third parties without compensating them, there are costs not represented in the market price of the good. If these external costs (or negative externalities) were included in the costs of producing the good, the market equilibrium price and quantity would reflect all the costs (both private and external) of the production of this good or its true social cost.

a. Using the following data, construct a worksheet to demonstrate a negative externality in the market for a good or service. The values for quantity should range from 0 to 130 in increments of 10. Calculate the price data for each quantity (Q) point using the demand relationship (P(Qd)), the supply relationship (P(Qs) or MPC), the cost of negative externality (EXT), and the marginal social cost relationship (P(Qs) + EXT or MSC).
   Input Area:

Q (Qd or Qs)	P(Qd)	P(Qs) or MPC	EXT	P(Qs)+EXT or MSC
0	=60-.5*Qd	=10+.5*Qs	$10	=(10+.5*Qs)+10 or
10				=20+.5*Qs
|				
130				

P(Qd) represents the market demand relationship expressed as price being a function of quantity.

P(Qs) is the market supply relationship expressed as price being a function of quantity and represents the marginal private cost (MPC) to produce the good.

EXT represents the value of the external cost per unit of the good produced, sold, or used.

MSC is the marginal social cost, which represents the sum of the marginal private cost (market supply) and the value of the externality (P(Qs)+EXT).

b.   Construct a line chart of the price data for P(Qd), P(Qs) (or MPC), EXT, and MSC (or P(Qs)+EXT). Label them D, S or MPC, EXT, and MSC, respectively. Use the quantity (Q) data for the x-axis.

c.   What will the market equilibrium price and quantity be for this good, given the private benefits and private costs represented by the market demand and supply?

d.   Suppose the producers compensated the people who bear the product's external costs. What would the market supply curve look like? What would happen to the equilibrium price and quantity in this market? What happens to consumer and producer surplus?

58.   POSITIVE EXTERNALITY

Note: The data for the values of quantity (Q), demand (P(Qd)), supply (P(Qs)), and the externality (EXT) are taken from assignment 57. Thus, a direct comparison can be made concerning the impact of positive and negative externalities in a given market.

When the production, sale, or use of a good or service confers benefits on third parties without the resource owners or producers being compensated, there are benefits not represented in the market price of the good. If these external benefits (or positive externality) were included in the demand for the good, the market equilibrium price and quantity would reflect all of the benefits (both private and external) of the production of this good or its true social benefit.

a.   Using the following data, construct a worksheet to demonstrate a positive externality in the market for a good or service. The values for quantity should range from 0 to 130 in increments of 10. Calculate the price data for each quantity (Q) point using the demand relationship (P(Qd)), the supply relationship (P(Qs)), the value of the positive externality (EXT), and the marginal social benefit relationship (MSB).

Input Area:

Q (Qd or Qs)	P(Qd) or MPB	P(Qs)	EXT	P(Qd)+EXT or MSB
0	=60-.5*Qd	=10+.5*Qs	$10	=(60-.5*Qd)+10 or
10				=70-.5*Qd
130				

P(Qd) or MPB represents the demand relationship or marginal private benefit (MPB). The market demand relationship represents the marginal private benefit because it indicates the additional value a consumer must obtain in order to voluntarily purchase each additional unit of the good.

P(Qs) represents the supply relationship.

EXT represents the value of the externality per unit.

MSB is the marginal social benefit, which represents the addition of marginal private benefit and external benefit (value) from each unit of the good (P(Qd)+EXT).

b. Construct a line chart of the price data for P(Qd) or MPB, P(Qs), EXT, and MSB. Label them D or MPB, S, EXT, and MSB respectively. Use the quantity (Q) data for the x-axis.

c. What is the market equilibrium price and quantity for this good, given the private benefits and private costs represented by the market demand and supply?

d. Suppose that the people receiving the external benefits of this product are compensating those purchasing the product for the benefit received from each unit purchased. What would the market demand curve look like? What would happen to the equilibrium price and quantity in this market? What would happen to consumer and producer surplus?

59. IMPACT OF AN IMPORT QUOTA*

An import quota is a legal limit set on the quantity of an imported good. A quota affects both domestic consumers and producers because the restriction on supply changes both the equilibrium price and quantity in the country imposing the quota.

a. Use the following data to construct a worksheet to demonstrate the effects of an import quota on the importing country. The value for quantity should range from 0 to 100 in increments of 10.

Q	P(Qd)	P(Qs)	Pw	Qim	P(Qs+Qim)
0	=55-.5*Qd	=5+.5*Qs	$20	20	= -5+.5*Qs or
10					= 5+.5*Qs-.5*Qim
100					

Q represents the quantity of the good exchanged and can be either quantity demanded (Qd) or quantity supplied (Qs).

P(Qd) represents the domestic demand relationship expressed as price being a function of quantity.

P(Qs) represents the domestic supply relationship expressed as price being a function of quantity.

Pw is the supply of this good to this economy that can be represented by an infinitely elastic supply at the world equilibrium price. It is important to note that there will not be any imports of the good if the domestic price is below the world price. However, as soon as the domestic market price reaches the world price, there is an unlimited additional supply available through importation.

Qim represents the imports that make up the difference between what the domestic suppliers provide at the world price and what the domestic demand is. Qim=Qd-Qs (at the world price). Thus, Qim can be calculated by simply setting the demand and supply relationships equal to the world price and determining the difference between Qd and Qs at the world price of $20 (70-30=40).

P(Qs+Qim) is the supply relationship including the quota. In the case of an import quota, the quantity imported is legally restricted, in this instance to 20. Since this imported quantity is available at any price equal to or above the world price, it can be portrayed as an increase in the supply of the good (a shift to the right) equal to the imported quantity (but only when price is above the world price).

Calculate the price for each quantity (Q) point given the demand relationship (P(Qd)) and the supply relationship (P(Qs)). Also calculate the price for each quantity point for all quantities at the world price and greater using the supply relationship plus the quota. Recall, at the world price of $20, Qs is 30 units and Qim is restricted to 20 units, so Qs+Qim is 50 units. Calculate the supply increase due to imports (P(Qs+Qim)) for all quantity points of 50 units or greater.

b.   Construct a line chart of the data for P(Qd), P(Qs), and P(Qs+Qim). Label them D, S, and S+Qim respectively. Use the quantity (Q) data for the x-axis.

c.   Referring to the line chart, if there were not an import quota, what would the equilibrium price and quantity be? With the quota of 20, what is the equilibrium price and quantity?

d.   Referring to the line chart, when an import quota is imposed, what happens to producer surplus in the importing country? Why?

e.   What happens to consumer surplus in the importing country as a result of the quota? Why? Which is larger, the gain in domestic producer surplus or the loss of domestic consumer surplus?

60.   IMPACT OF AN IMPORT QUOTA

An import quota is a legal limit set on the quantity of an imported good. A quota affects both domestic consumers and producers because the restriction on supply changes both the equilibrium price and quantity in the country imposing the quota.

a.   Use the data provided below to construct a worksheet to demonstrate the effects of the increase in an import quota on the importing country. In this case, increasing a quota represents allowing more importation of a good (i.e., a reduction in a trade restriction). The value for quantity should range from 0 to 100 in increments of 5.

Input Area:

Q	P(Qd)	P(Qs)	Pw	Qim	P(Qs+Qim)	Q'im	P'(Qs+Qim')
0	=120-Qd	=20+Qs	$50	20	=Qs or	30	= -10+Qs or
10					=20+Qs-Qim		=20+Qs-Qim'
|							
100							

Q represents the quantity of the good exchanged and can be either quantity demanded (Qd) or quantity supplied (Qs).

P(Qd) represents the domestic demand relationship expressed as price being a function of quantity.

P(Qs) represents the domestic supply relationship expressed as price being a function of quantity.

Pw is the supply of this good to this economy that can be represented by an infinitely elastic supply at the world equilibrium price. It is important to note that there will not be any imports of the good if the domestic price is below the world price. However, as soon as the domestic market price reaches the world price, there is an unlimited additional supply available through importation.

Qim represents the imports that make up the difference between what the domestic suppliers provide at the world price and what the domestic demand is. Qim=Qd-Qs (at the world price).

P(Qs+Qim) is the supply relationship including the quota. In the case of an import quota, the quantity imported is equally restricted, in this instance to 20. Since this imported quantity is available at any price equal to or above the world price, it can be portrayed as an increase in the supply of the good (a shift to the right) equal to the imported quantity (but only when price is above the world price).

Qim' represents an increase in the quota.

P'(Qs+Qim') is the new supply relationship including the increased quota.

Calculate the price for each quantity (Q) point given the demand relationship (P(Qd)), the supply relationship (P(Qs)), the supply relationship plus the quota (P(Qs+Qim)), and the supply relationship plus the increased quota (P'(Qs+Qim')). At the world price of $20, Qs is 30 units and Qim is restricted to 20 units, so Qs+Qim is 50 units. Calculate the supply relationship plus the original quota for all quantity points of 50 or greater since this represents the prices at or above the world price. Similarly, supply relationship plus the increased quota is calculated for quantity points of 60 and greater (Qs=30, Qim'=30).

b. Construct a line chart of the data for P(Qd), P(Qs), P(Qs+Qim), and P'(Qs+Qim'). Label them D, S, S+Qim, and S+Qim', respectively. Use the quantity (Q) data for the x-axis.

c. Referring to the line chart, what is the equilibrium price and quantity for each of the quotas?

d. Would consumers or producers be more likely to favor increasing the quota? Why?

e. What happens to consumer and producer surplus as a result of the increased quota? Explain.

61. IMPACT OF A TARIFF

Note: The data for quantity (Q), the demand relationship expressed as price being a function of quantity (P(Qd)), the supply relationship expressed as price being a function of quantity (P(Qs)), and the world price (Pw) are taken from assignment 59. This allows the comparison of the impact of a tariff to that of an import quota.

A tariff is a tax placed on goods imported into a country. The simplest is a flat tax per unit. This type of tariff will be used to demonstrate the impact of a tax on both consumers and producers in the importing country. As the trade restriction reduces the available supply at each market price, both equilibrium price and quantity will be changed in the country imposing the tariff.

a. Use the following data to construct a worksheet that demonstrates the effects of an import tariff in the importing country. The value for quantity should range from 0 to 100 in increments of 10. Calculate the price data for each quantity point using the demand relationship (P(Qd)), the supply relationship (P(Qs)), the world price (Pw), and the world price including the tariff (Pw+T).

Input Area:

Q	P(Qd)	P(Qs)	Pw	T	Pw+T
0	=55-.5*Qd	=5+.5*Qs	$20	$5	$25
10					
100					

T represents the tariff per unit.

b.   Construct a line chart for P(Qd), P(Qs), Pw, and Pw+T. Label them D, S, Pw, and Pw+T, respectively. Use the quantity data (Q) for the x-axis.

c.   What is the equilibrium price and quantity for this good before the tariff and after the tariff is impc_ed?

d.   When the results of a quota of 20 (from assignment 58) and a tariff of $5 are compared in this same market, the results are similar. The primary distinction between the results of the two has to do with the disposition of the loss in consumer surplus. How many units are imported after the tariff is imposed? How much tax revenue does the government receive from consumers as a result of the tariff? In cases where some importation of the good is permitted, which method of restriction is most likely preferred by government, a tariff or a quota? Why?

62.   IMPACT OF A TARIFF

Note: The data for quantity (Q), the demand relationship expressed as price being a function of quantity (P(Qd)), the supply relationship expressed as price being a function of quantity (P(Qs)), and the world price (Pw) are taken from assignment 60. This allows the comparison of the impact of a tariff to that of an import quota.

A tariff is a tax placed on goods imported into a country. The simplest is a flat tax per unit. This type of tariff will be used to demonstrate the impact of a tax on both consumers and producers in the importing country. As the trade restriction reduces the available supply at each market price, both equilibrium price and quantity will be changed in the country imposing the tariff.

a.   Use the following data to construct a worksheet that demonstrates the effects of increasing a tariff in the importing country. The value for quantity should range from 0 to 100 in increments of 5. Calculate the price data for each quantity point using the demand relationship (P(Qd)), the supply relationship (P(Qs)), the world price (Pw), the world price including the tariff (Pw+T), and the world price with the increased tariff (Pw+T').

Input Area:

Q	P(Qd)	P(Qs)	Pw	T	Pw+T	T'	Pw+T'	TRev
0	=120-Qd	=20+Qs	$50	$10	$60	$15	$65	=T*Qim
5								
100								

T represents the tariff per unit.

T' represents the increased tariff per unit.

TRev =T*Qim, where Qim (quantity imported) is the difference between Qd and
      Qs at the <u>effective</u> world price (Pw + tariff).

b.   Construct a line chart of the data for P(Qd), P(Qs), Pw, Pw+T, and Pw+T'. Label them D, S, Pw, Pw+T, and Pw+T', respectively. Use quantity data for the x-axis.

c.   What is the equilibrium price at the original tariff (T) and at the increased tariff (T')? What happens to consumer surplus and producer surplus as a result of this increase in the tariff?

d.   What is the tax revenue generated at each of these tariffs? Explain why revenue changed in this way.

63.   FOREIGN EXCHANGE RATE

The foreign exchange rate of a currency is the price of that currency in terms of another currency. For example, the exchange rate of the euro would be the amount of dollars and cents one would need to pay in exchange for a single euro ($/euro). In an era of essentially floating exchange rates, the price of a euro is largely determined in the foreign exchange markets around the world. The forces of supply and demand cause their market prices to adjust toward an equilibrium exchange rate (price) and quantity as the supply and demand for this currency changes on a continuing basis.

a.   Use the data provided below to construct a worksheet that demonstrates how a foreign exchange market attains an equilibrium exchange rate and how the equilibrium is affected by a change in demand for this currency (or a change in the supply of this currency). The value for quantity (Q euro) should range from 0 to 100 in increments of 10. Calculate the euro exchange rate in dollars for each quantity point using the demand relationship (P(Qd euro)), the supply relationship (P(Qs euro)), and the new demand relationship (P'(Qd euro)).

Q euro	P(Qd euro)	P(Qs euro)	P'(Qd euro)
0	=1.5-.01*Qd euro	=.3+.01*Qs euro	=1.9-.01*Qd euro
10			
100			

Q euro represents the quantity of euro in millions.
P(Qd euro) represents the initial demand for euros in exchange for dollars.
P(Qs euro) represents the initial supply of euros in exchange for dollars.
P'(Qd euro) represents a change in demand for euros in exchange for dollars.

b.   Construct a line chart of the data for P(Qd euro), P(Qs euro), and P'(Qd euro). Label them D euro, S euro, and D' euro, respectively. Use the quantity (Q euro) data for the x-axis. Note: The y-axis will be in terms of dollars per euro or $/euro.

c.   What will be the initial equilibrium exchange rate and quantity of euros exchanged?

d.   When the demand changes to D' euro, what happens to the equilibrium exchange rate for euros and the quantity exchanged? Has the value of the euro increased or decreased? What has happened to the value of the dollar?

64.   FOREIGN EXCHANGE RATE

The foreign exchange rate of a currency is the price of that currency in terms of another currency. For example, the exchange rate of the euro would be the amount of dollars and cents one would need to pay in exchange for a single euro ($/euro). In an era of essentially floating exchange rates, the price of a euro is largely determined in the foreign exchange markets around the world. The forces of supply and demand cause their market prices to adjust toward an equilibrium exchange rate (price) and quantity as the supply and demand for this currency changes on a continuing basis.

a.   Use the data provided below to construct a worksheet that demonstrates how a foreign exchange market attains an equilibrium exchange rate and how the equilibrium is affected by a subsequent change in both the demand and supply for this currency. The value for quantity (Q euro) should range from 0 to 100 in increments of 10. Calculate the euro exchange rate in dollars for each quantity point using the initial demand relationship (P(Qd euro)), the initial supply relationship (P(Qs euro)), the subsequent demand relationship (P'(Qd euro)), and the subsequent supply relationship (P(Qs euro)).

Input Area:

Q euro	P(Qd euro)	P(Qs euro)	P'(Qd euro)	P'(Qs euro)
0	=1.3-.01*Qd euro	=.5+.01*Qs euro	=1.55-.01*Qd euro	=.55+.01*Qs euro
10				
|				
100				

Q euro represents the quantity of euro in millions.
P(Qd euro) represents the initial demand for euros in exchange for dollars.
P(Qs euro) represents the initial supply of euros in exchange for dollars.

P'(Qd euro) represents the subsequent demand for euros in exchange for dollars.
P'(Qs euro) represents the subsequent supply of euros in exchange for dollars.

b. Construct a line chart of the data for P(Qd euro), P(Qs euro), P'(Qd euro), and P'(Qs euro). Label them D euro, S euro, D' euro, and S' euro, respectively. Use the quantity (Q euro) data for the x-axis. Note: The y-axis will be in terms of dollars per euro or $/euro.

c. What will be the initial equilibrium exchange rate and quantity of euros exchanged? Suppose the American stock market prices fell significantly as well as interest rates on bonds and savings accounts, but those effects were less in Europe. What would likely happen to the supply and demand in the euro exchange market?

d. After the demand and supply of euros changed to D' euro and S' euro, what happened to the equilibrium exchange rate and quantity of euros exchanged? What has happened to the value of the euro? What has happened to the value of the dollar?

65. COMPARATIVE ADVANTAGE*

The law of comparative advantage is the basis for understanding specialization and trade. The gains from trade that result from differing opportunity costs in production can be illustrated by using a simple two person, two good example. Linear production possibilities curves can be used to demonstrate the law of comparative advantage.

a. Using the data provided below, construct a worksheet to illustrate the production possibilities of two individuals (Rene and Jean) in producing haircuts and shampoos in an eight-hour work day. The purpose is to demonstrate the gains if specialization in accordance with comparative advantage occurs.

Input Area:

QAr	QBr	QAj	QBj	QAr(QB)	QAj(QB)	QAr(QB)+QAj(QB)	QA(QB)
10	20	20	10	=10-.5*QB	=20-2*QB	=30-QB	=20-QB

QAr represents the quantity of good A (haircuts) that Rene can accomplish in 8 hours if she does haircuts only.
QBr represents the quantity of good B (shampoos) that Rene can accomplish in eight hours if she does shampoos only.
QAj represents the quantity of good A (haircuts) that Jean can accomplish in eight hours doing only haircuts.
QBj represents the quantity of good B (shampoos) that Jean can accomplish in eight hours doing only shampoos.
QAr(QB) and QAj(QB) represent the production possibilities for Rene and Jean, respectively. From the data given and using a linear relationship for the

quantities of good A based on how many units of good B are produced, one can determine their production possibilities.

QAr(QB)+QAj(QB) is the addition of what Rene and Jean can produce if they spend the same amount of time doing good A and then spend the rest of their time performing good B.

QA(QB), or the exchange ratio of good A in terms of good B, which represents the fact that haircuts (good A) and shampoos (good B) have the same price.

The maximum number of shampoos (good B) Rene and Jean can produce in eight hours is 30 (QBr+QBj). Use this information to construct a data set listing possible quantity points for good B from 0 to 30 in increments of 2. Label this data set QB. Using the QB data and the relationships provided, calculate the quantities of good A that Rene and Jean could each produce if they individually produced the amount of good B indicated by QB (up to the maximum they each can do in eight hours) using QAr(QB) and QAj(QB) respectively. Calculate their combined production of good A at each quantity B (QB) point if they each spent the same proportions of their time on those two goods (QAr(QB)+QAj(QB)).

b. Determine which individual has the lowest opportunity cost (gives up the least amount of the other good for each unit produced) for good A and who has the lowest opportunity cost for good B. Assuming they try to specialize in what they have comparative advantage in, determine how much of good A they will produce at each quantity B (QB) point. Label this QArj(QB). From QB=0 to QB=20, Rene will be producing all of the good B specified at each point while Jean produces only good A. Why?

From the good B quantity point of 20 to 30, Jean will have to produce the additional good B. What happens to the tradeoff in terms of the reduction of good A produced in order to increase good B production?

c. Calculate the data for QA(QB) at each quantity of B point (QB). Construct a line chart for the data from QAr(QB), QAj(QB), QAr(QB)+QAj(QB), QArj(QB), and QA(QB). Label them PPFr, PPFj, PPFr+PPFj, PPFrj, and CPC, respectively. Use the quantity of B data (QB) for the x-axis. The y-axis is the quantity of A.
Note: CPC means consumption possibilities curve. It shows what can be produced if each person specializes in her job and then trades tasks one for one (the price ratio).

d. Comparing PPFr+PPFj to PPFrj, what is occurring in terms of the joint production with and without specialization in accordance with comparative advantage? What is the incentive for Rene and Jean to specialize in accordance with comparative advantage?

e.   Suppose that good A and good B have the same value in exchange (sell for the same market price) as shown by CPC. Presume that Rene and Jean are paid through commission and tips and that each had customers who wanted both a shampoo and haircut in the same visit. If they traded one for one doing the shampoos or haircuts for each other in accordance with comparative advantage, what would the CPC demonstrate about the number of each type of good they would be paid for?

66.   INTERNATIONAL COMPARATIVE ADVANTAGE

An issue one can debate is whether a small, relatively underdeveloped country can gain from specializing and trading with more developed countries, or would it be better off not to enter into international trade and seek to develop self-sufficiency within its own economy. The application of the law of comparative advantage demonstrates the answer to this issue. A two nation, two good example along with linear production possibilities curves can be used to demonstrate how international trade in accordance with comparative advantage will affect both the lesser developed and the more developed country.

a.   Using the data provided below, construct a worksheet in order to create the production possibilities curves for two nations, with one nation having an absolute advantage in the production of both goods compared to the other country.

Input Area:

QAi	QBi	QAus	QBus	QAi(QB)	QAus(QB)	QA(QB)i	QA(QB)us
20	10	25	75	=20-2*QB	=25-.333*QB	=20-.5*QB	=37.5-.5*(QB)

QAi is the maximum quantity of good A (oil) that can be produced by Iran.

QBi is the maximum quantity of good B (grain) that can be produced by Iran.

QAus and QBus are the maximum quantities of good A and good B, respectively, that can be produced by the U.S.

QAi(QB) and QAus(QB) represent the tradeoff between goods A and B in production by Iran and the U.S., respectively. The relationship is expressed as the quantity of oil (QA) in millions of barrels being a function of how much grain in millions of tons is produced.

QA(QB)i and QA(QB)us represent the consumption possibilities curves (CPC) for Iran and the U.S. respectively. These reflect an exchange ratio of two units of grain for each unit of oil as shown by the slope of -.5. This exchange ratio was chosen to be somewhere between the opportunity costs of production of these two countries as specified above (QAi(QB) and QAus(QB)).

Since the maximum number of units of good B either country can produce is 75 units, construct a data set for the quantity of good B (QB) from 0 to 80 in increments of 5. For each quantity point of B (QB), calculate the quantity of A data using QAi(QB), QAus(QB), QA(QB)i, and QA(QB)us.

b. Construct a line chart of the quantity of good A data for QAi(QB), QAus(QB), QA(QB)i, and QA(QB)us. Label these PPFi, PPFus, CPCi, and CPCus, respectively. Use the quantity of good B data (QB) for the x-axis and label the y-axis as "Quantity of Good A."

c. Suppose Iran decides to specialize in accordance with comparative advantage; which good will it produce and trade to get the other? Why? Assume Iran needs 10 units of good A for its domestic consumption, how much more of good B will it have if it specializes and trades rather than produces both goods for its domestic use?

d. Suppose the U.S. decides to specialize in the good it has comparative advantage in. What will it specialize in? Assume the U.S. needs 20 units of good A for its domestic consumption. How much more of good B will the U.S. have if it specializes and trades, rather than producing both goods for its own use? Some would say that since the U.S. can produce more of good A and good B than Iran (has an absolute advantage), there is no reason for the U.S. to specialize and trade. How does the application of the law of comparative advantage refute such a statement?

e. According to the law of comparative advantage, will Iran gain or lose by specializing and trading internationally? If Iran attempts to become self-sufficient, what will happen to its consumption of these two goods?

Solutions to Selected Assignments

1.   Real versus nominal prices, p.106
3.   Supply and demand, p.107
4.   Change in demand, p.109
8.   Price elasticity coefficient of demand, p.111
16.   Indifference curves, p.113
19.   Utility analysis, p.115
21.   Production function, p.118
22.   Total marginal product, p.121
26.   Unit cost and revenue analysis, p.124
30.   Profit analysis, p.126
35.   Short run supply for the perfect competitor, p.130
44.   Monopolist profit, p.133
51.   Present value, p.136
54.   Production possibility frontier (curve), p.137
59.   Impact of an import quota, p.139
65.   Comparative advantage, p.141

1. REAL VERSUS NOMINAL PRICES

Calculate the real price of milk in 1980 dollars and in 1990 dollars by inserting the appropriate formula into your worksheet.

FILE IDENTIFICATION AREA
Filename: Real Price # 1
Designer: Mike Duke
Input Required:
  a. market price per unit (P) at selected time periods
  c. Consumer Price Index (CPI) data with base year 1980 for the same time periods
  b. Consumer Price Index (CPI) data with base year 1990 for the same time periods
  d. market/ real price relationship
Output: real prices for the time periods of the market prices using CPI's with alternate base years
File Created:
File Modified:

INPUT AREA:

Year:	1980	1985	1990	1995	1998
P:	$1.05	$1.13	$1.39	$1.48	$1.61
CPI(1980$):	100.00	130.58	158.62	184.95	197.82
CPI(1990$):	63.04	82.34	100.00	116.60	124.71

market /real price relationship: real P=(P/CPI)*100

OUTPUT AREA:

P:	$1.05	$1.13	$1.39	$1.48	$1.61
real P(1980$):	$1.05	$0.87	$0.88	$0.80	$0.81
real P(1990$):	$1.67	$1.37	$1.39	$1.27	$1.29

Formulas (relationships) used in output area:
real price in 1980 $'s (real P(1980$)): Calculated where real P=(P/CPI(1980$))*100
real price in 1990 $'s (real P(1990$)): Calculated where real P=(P/CPI(1990$))*100

3. SUPPLY AND DEMAND

a,b. Worksheet

FILE IDENTIFICATION AREA
Filename: Supply and Demand # 3
Designer: Mike Duke
Input Required: P, Qd, Qs, Q, P(Qd), P(Qs)
Output: Supply and Demand Schedules
 a. quantity demanded at market prices (Qd)
 b. quantity supplied at market prices (Qs)
File Created:

INPUT AREA:

P	Qd	Qs	Q	P(Qd)	P(Qs)
$0	=110-2*P	=-10+2*P	0	=55-.5*Qd	=5+.5*Qs
$5			10		
$10			20		
$15			30		
$20			40		
$25			50		
$30			60		
$35			70		
$40			80		
$45			90		
$50			100		
			110		
			120		
			130		

OUTPUT AREA:

P	Qd	Qs	Q	P(Qd)	P(Qs)
$0	110	-10	0	$55	$5
$5	100	0	10	$50	$10
$10	90	10	20	$45	$15
$15	80	20	30	$40	$20
$20	70	30	40	$35	$25
$25	60	40	**50**	**$30**	**$30**
$30	**50**	**50**	60	$25	$35
$35	40	60	70	$20	$40
$40	30	70	80	$15	$45
$45	20	80	90	$10	$50
$50	10	90	100	$5	$55
			110	$0	$60
			120	-$5	$65
			130	-$10	$70

At what price and quantity will the market be in equilibrium?
Answer: P=$30, Q=50

3c.   Supply and demand line chart

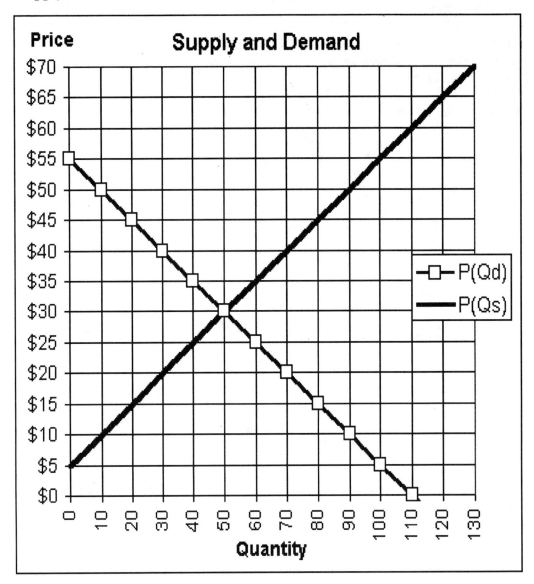

d.   **Determine the market equilibrium price and quantity. Compare the results with the values calculated in part a.**
Answer: The values are the same: P=$30, Q=50

4. CHANGE IN DEMAND
a. Worksheet

FILE IDENTIFICATION AREA
Filename: Supply and Demand # 4
Designer: Mike Duke
Input Required:
        a. Market prices (P)
        b. Demand relationship
        c. Supply relationship
        d. Quantity (Q)
Output: Supply and Demand Schedules
        a. quantity demanded at market prices (Qd)
        b. quantity supplied at market prices (Qs)
File Created:
File Modified:
File Last Used:

INPUT AREA:

P	Qd	Qs	Q	P(Qd)	P(Qs)
$0	=165-.6*P	=-37.50+.75*P	0	=275-(5/3)*Qd	=50+(4/3)*Qs
$10			25		
$20			50		
$30			75		
$40			100		
$50			125		
$60			150		
$70			175		
$80					
$90					
$100					

OUTPUT AREA:

P	Qd	Qs	Q	P(Qd)	P(Qs)
$0	$165	-$37.50	0	$275.00	$50.00
$10	$159	-$30.00	25	$233.33	$83.33
$20	$153	-$22.50	50	$191.67	$116.67
$30	$147	-$15.00	75	$150.00	$150.00
$40	$141	-$7.50	100	$108.33	$183.33
$50	$135	$0.00	125	$66.67	$216.67
$60	$129	$7.50	150	$25.00	$250.00
$70	$123	$15.00	175	-$16.67	$283.33
$80	$117	$22.50			
$90	$111	$30.00			
$100	$105	$37.50			

4b.   **Line chart**

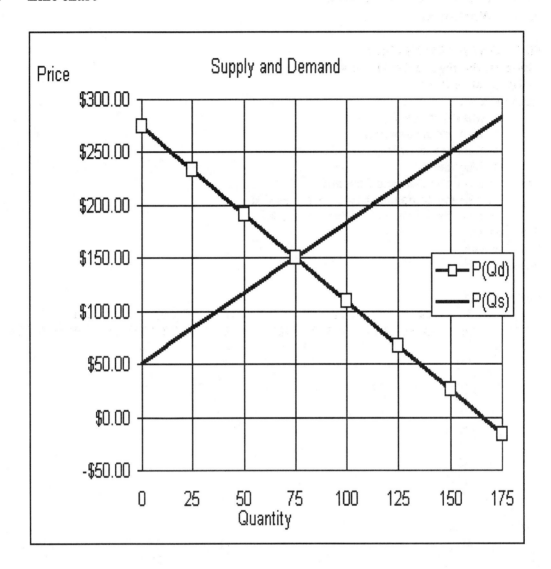

What is the equilibrium price and quantity?
Answer: Equilibrium price is $150 at a quantity of 75 units.

c.   **Suppose the formula for P(Qd) changes to:**   **P(Qd)=200 - (5/3)*Qd. What is the new equilibrium price and quantity?**
Answer: New equilibrium is 116.75 at a quantity of 50 units.

8. PRICE ELASTICITY COEFFICIENT OF DEMAND
a. Worksheet (File ID and Input Area)

FILE IDENTIFICATION AREA

Filename: Price Elasticity Coefficient of Demand # 8

Designer: Mike Duke

Input Required:

        a. demand relationship: Qd(P)

        b. price as a function of quantity relationship: P(Qd) or AR (average revenue)

        c. quantity demanded: Qd or Q

        d. price elasticity of demand relationship: PEC(D)

        e. total revenue relationship: TR

        f. marginal revenue relationship: MR

Output: Price elasticity of demand

        a. quantity demanded at market prices: Q or Qd

        b. market price (average revenue) at quantities demanded: P(Qd) or AR

        c. marginal revenue at quantities demanded: MR

        c. price elasticity of demand at quanties demanded: PEC(D)

File Created:

File Modified:

File Last Used:

INPUT AREA:

Qd	P(Qd)	Q (or Qd)	PEC(D)	TR	MR
=155-P	=155-Q	0	=P/(P-VID)	TR=P*Q or	MR=((P_{i+1}*Q_{i+1})-
		10		=155*Q-Q^2	(P_i*Q_i))/(Q_{i+1}-Q_i)
		20			
		30			
		40			
		50			
		60			
		70			
		80			
		90			
		100			
		110			
		120			
		130			
		140			

8a.   Worksheet (Output Area)

OUTPUT AREA:

Q	P(Qd)	TR	MR	PEC(D)
0	155	0		
10	145	1450	145	-14.5
20	135	2700	125	-6.8
30	125	3750	105	-4.2
40	115	4600	85	-2.9
50	105	5250	65	-2.1
60	95	5700	45	-1.6
70	85	5950	25	-1.2
80	75	6000	5	-0.9
90	65	5850	-15	-0.7
100	55	5500	-35	-0.6
110	45	4950	-55	-0.4
120	35	4200	-75	-0.3
130	25	3250	-95	-0.2
140	15	2100	-115	-0.1

b.   Price elasticity coefficient of demand line chart

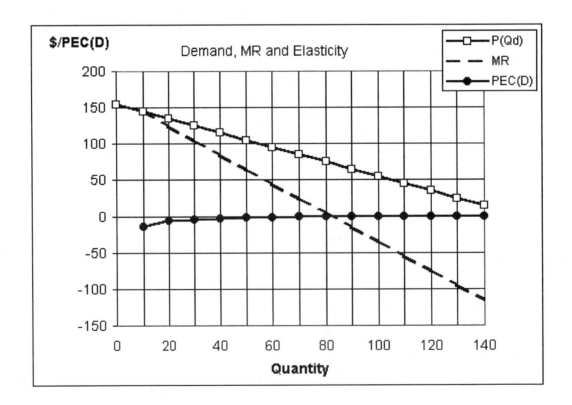

16.   INDIFFERENCE CURVES
a.   Worksheet

FILE IDENTIFICATION AREA
Filename: Indifference Curves # 16
Designer: Mike Duke
Input Required:
  a. quantity of good B: Q(B)

  b. indifference quantities for good A for each specified level of good B for utility level 1: $Q(A)@I_1$

  c. indifference quantities for good A for each specified level of good B for utility level 2: $Q(A)@I_2$
Output :
  a. quantity of good B: Q(B)

  b. indifference quantities for good A for each specified level of good B for utility level 1: $Q(A)@I_1$

  c. indifference quantities for good A for each specified level of good B for utility level 2: $Q(A)@I_2$
File Created:
File Modified:
File Last Used:

INPUT AREA:

Q(B)	$Q(A)@I_1$	$Q(A)@I_2$
0		
4	46	60
8	22	30
12	9	16
16	4	7.5
20	3.4	5
24	2.9	4.3
28	2.5	3.8
32	2.2	3.5
36	2	3.3
40	1.9	3.2

OUTPUT AREA:

Q(B)	$Q(A)@I_1$	$Q(A)@I_2$
0		
4	46	60
8	22	30
12	9	16
16	4	7.5
20	3.4	5
24	2.9	4.3
28	2.5	3.8
32	2.2	3.5
36	2	3.3
40	1.9	3.2

16b. Line chart

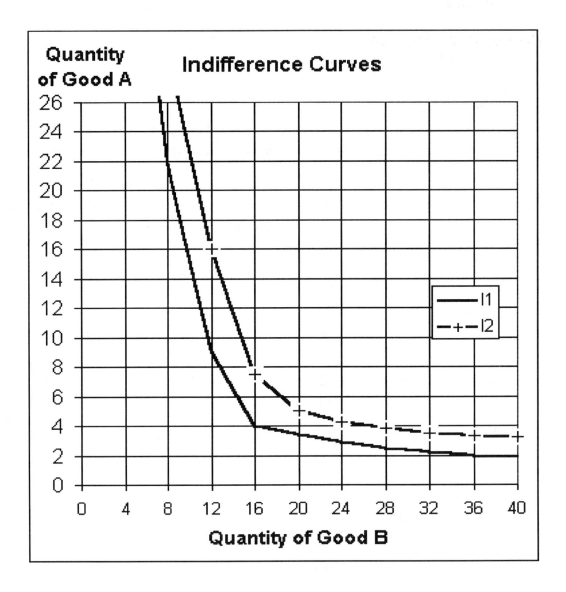

c. **Why is it reasonable to believe that I_2 represents a higher level of utility than I_1?** Answer: Because I_2 is composed of combinations of good A and good B that represents larger quantities than any of the combinations represented in I_1.

d. **What principle of indifference curves does the shape of I_1 and I_2 demonstrate that is related to diminishing marginal utility?**
Answer: I_1 and I_2 are both convex from the origin, demonstrating a falling marginal rate of substitution as the quantity of either good is increased. This is the logical result of the law of diminishing marginal utility.

19.   UTILITY ANALYSIS
a.   Worksheet (File ID)

FILE IDENTIFICATION AREA
Filename: Utility Analysis # 19
Designer: Mike Duke
Input Required:

a. quantity of good A: Q(A)
b. total utility relationship for good A: TU(A)
c. average utility relationship for good A: AU(A)
d. marginal utility relationship for good A: MU(A)
e. market price of good A: P(A)
f. quantity of good B: Q(B)
g. total utility relationship for good B: TU(B)
h. average utility relationship for good B: AU(B)
i. marginal utility relationship for good B: MU(B)
j. market price of good A: P(A)
k. budget (income) relationship (consumer equilibrium condition)
l. income: Y

Output :

a. quantity of good A : Q(A)
b. total utility for good A (TU(A)) at each quantity
c. marginal utility for good A (MU(A)) at each quantity
d. market price of good A: P(A)
e. marginal utility per dollar for good A: MU(A)/P(A)
f. quantity of good B: Q(B)
g. total utility for good B (TU(B)) at each quantity
h. marginal utility for good B (MU(B)) at each quantity
i. market price of good B: P(B)
j. marginal utility per dollar for good B: MU(B)/P(B)
k. budget (income): Y=$75=(P(A)*Q(A))+(P(B)*Q(B))

File Created:
File Modified:
File Last Used:

19a. Worksheet (Input and Output Areas)

INPUT AREA:

Q(A)	P(A)	TU(A)	MU(A)	Q(B)	P(B)	TU(B)	MU(B)
0	$5	=105*Q(A) -	=105-10*Q(A)	0	$10	=42*Q(B) -	=42-4*Q(B)
1		5*(Q(A)^2)		1		2*(Q(B)^2)	
2				2			
3				3			
4				4			Y
5				5		$75≥(P(A)*Q(A))+(P(B)*Q(B))	
6				6			
7				7			
8				8			
9				9			
10				10			
11				11			

OUTPUT AREA:

Q(A)	TU(A)	MU(A)	P(A)	MU(A)/P(A)	Q(B)	TU(B)	MU(B)	P(B)	MU(B)/P(B)	Y
0	0		$5		0	0		$10		$75≥($5*9) +
1	100	105		21.0	1	38	42		4.2	($10*3)
2	190	95		19.0	2	68	38		3.8	
3	270	85		17.0	**3**	90	34		**3.4**	
4	340	75		15.0	4	104	30		3.0	
5	400	65		13.0	5	110	26		2.6	
6	450	55		11.0	6	108	22		2.2	
7	490	45		9.0	7	98	18		1.8	
8	520	35		7.0	8	80	14		1.4	
9	540	25		**5.0**	9	54	10		1.0	
10	550	15		3.0	10	20	6		0.6	
11	550	5		1.0	11	-22	2		0.2	

b.   **If you have $75 to spend (your income or budget limit), how much of each product would you buy to maximize your total utility? Why would this be the best way to maximize your utility from buying these two goods with your total budget of $75?**
Answer: With $75 to spend, to maximize utility, you would first buy 9 units of Product A at a cost of $45. The ninth unit provided MUA/PA of 5. Next, you would purchase 3 units of Product B at a cost of $30. The third unit of Product B provided MUB/PB of 3.4. Thus, you would purchase a total of 9 units of A for $45 and three units of B for $30.
What rule was used?
Answer: The rule is that the ratio of marginal utility to price will be equal for each good at equilibrium. To arrive at this equilibrium condition, incrementally purchase units of each good according to the marginal utility per dollar until the budget constraint is reached.

19c. Line charts

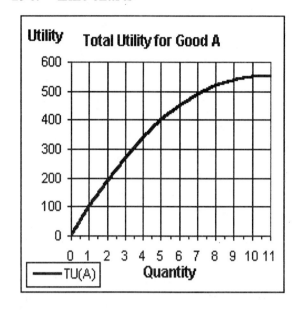

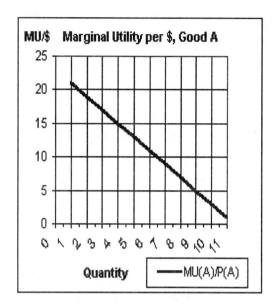

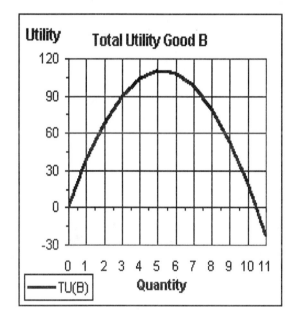

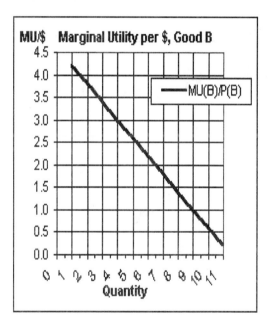

How do the marginal utility per dollar charts show that the quantity selected for each good is the best that can be done with $75?

Answer: As the decision to buy a unit of good A or good B is made, the MU/$ chart shows the utility per dollar that each will yield given all earlier units purchased. As long as each unit purchased results in the highest utility per dollar when the budget has been expended, the outcome must be that each purchase resulted in the most utility per dollar.

21.   PRODUCTION FUNCTION
a.   Worksheet (File ID and Input Area)

FILE IDENTIFICATION AREA
Filename: Production Function # 21
Designer: Mike Duke
Input Required:

a. quantity of good A (fixed factor/input): Q(A)

b. quantity of good B (variable factor/input): Q(B)

c. total physical product showing output of good Y for combinations
of Q(A) and Q(B): TPP

d. increased quantity of good A (fixed factor/input): Q'(A)

e. total physical product showing output of good Y for combinations Q'(A) and Q(B): TPP

Output :

a. quantity of good A, a constant : Q(A)

b. quantity of good B (variable factor/input): Q(B)

c. total physical product of output of good Y for combinations of good A and B: TPP

d. increased quantity of good A (fixed factor/input): Q'(A)

e. total physical product showing output of good Y for combinations Q'(A) and Q(B): TPP

File Created:
File Modified:
File Last Used:

INPUT AREA:

Q(A)	Q(B)	TPP	Q'(A)	TPP'
40	0	0	50	0
	5	5		5.5
	10	11		12
	15	20		21.5
	20	33.5		36
	25	49		54
	30	63		70
	35	73		83
	40	80		92
	45	85		99
	50	88		102.5
	55	90		105
	60	91		106.5
	65	90		107

21a. **Worksheet (Output Area)**

OUTPUT AREA:

Q(A)	Q(B)	TPP	Q'(A)	TPP'
40	0	0	50	0
40	5	5	50	5.5
40	10	11	50	12
40	15	20	50	21.5
40	20	33.5	50	36
40	25	49	50	54
40	30	63	50	70
40	35	73	50	83
40	40	80	50	92
40	45	85	50	99
40	50	88	50	102.5
40	55	90	50	105
40	60	91	50	106.5
40	65	90	50	107

b. **Production function line chart**

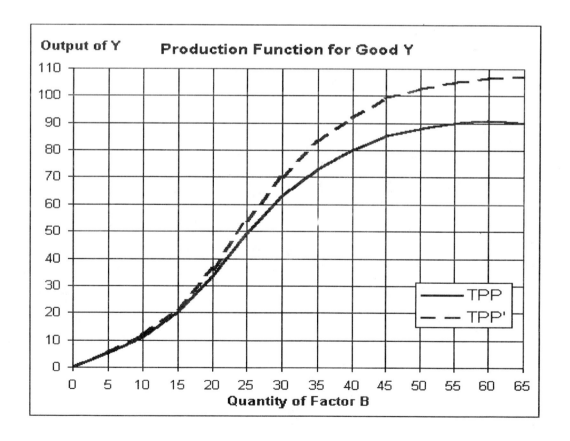

21c. **Why does the production function reach some maximum output in the short run as the variable factor is increased? At what level of Q(B) does TPP reach its maximum?**

Answer: As the variable factor is increased, the amount of the fixed factor becomes shorter in availability. At some point, adding more of the variable factor will not increase output due to a lack of the fixed factor in the process. TPP reaches its maximum in the vicinity of 60 units of factor B.

d. **If production is reconfigured with more of the fixed factor A, what would likely happen to output at any level of the variable factor B?**

Answer: We would expect that output for any given quantity of B would be greater than before the fixed factor was increased.

e. **What would happen to quantity of the variable factor B where the production function would reach its maximum?**

Answer: It would occur at a larger quantity of B than before.

22. TOTAL AND MARGINAL PRODUCT
a. Worksheet

FILE IDENTIFICATION AREA
Filename: Total and Marginal Product # 22
Designer: Mike Duke
Input: a. quantity of good A (fixed factor/input): Q(A)
                b. quantity of good B (variable factor/input): Q(B)
                c. total physical product showing output of good Y for combinations of A and B: TPP
                d. marginal physical product relationship for good B (the variable factor): MPP
Output :   a. quantity of good A, a constant : Q(A)
                b. quantity of good B (variable factor/input): Q(B)
                c. total physical product of output of good Y for combinations of good A and B: TPP
                d. marginal physical product for good B (the variable factor/resource) for all
                        combinations of good A and B: MPP

INPUT AREA:

Q(A)	Q(B)	TPP	MPP
40	0	0	$=(TPP_i - TPP_{i-1})/(Q(B)_i - Q(B)_{i-1})$
	5	5	
	10	11	
	15	20	
	20	33.5	
	25	49	
	30	63	
	35	73	
	40	80	
	45	85	
	50	88	
	55	90	
	60	91	
	65	90	

OUTPUT AREA:

Q(A)	Q(B)	TPP	MPP
40	0	0	
40	5	5	1.0
40	10	11	1.2
40	15	20	1.8
40	20	33.5	2.7
40	25	49	3.1
40	30	63	2.8
40	35	73	2.0
40	40	80	1.4
40	45	85	1.0
40	50	88	0.6
40	55	90	0.4
40	60	91	0.2
40	65	90	-0.2

22b. **What do you notice about the MPP when Q(B) is 65?**
Answer: MPP is negative, meaning that output actually decreased as the firm increased the use of the variable input.

c. **Line charts**

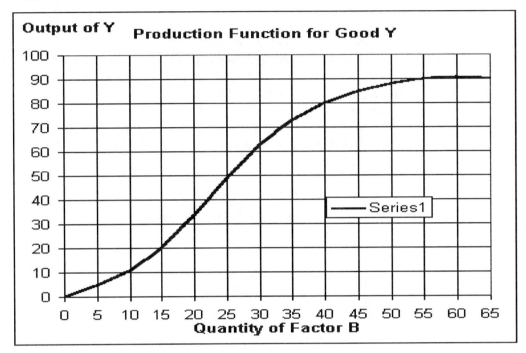

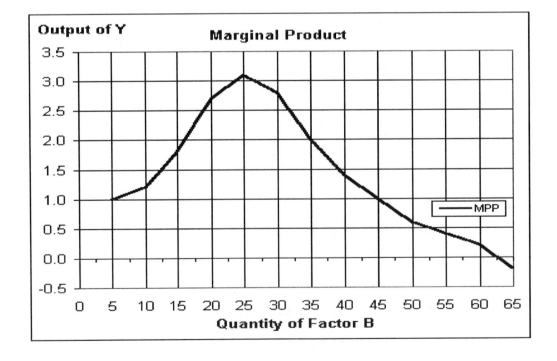

22d. **Suppose production is at an output level 33.5 where 20 units of the variable factor B are being used. Should output remain at this level given what the MPP data reveals? What is noticeable about MPP in the range of variable factor use from 0 to 25?**

Answer: Output should not remain at this level. If the use of factor B is increased, the additional output would be greater than for any of the previous units of B. MPP is increasing; this is called increasing returns.

e. **What is noticeable about MPP in the range of variable factor use from 25 to 60?** Answer: MPP is decreasing; this called diminishing returns.

26. UNIT COST AND REVENUE ANALYSIS

a. Worksheet

FILE IDENTIFICATION AREA

Filename: Unit Cost and Revenue Analysis # 26

Designer: Mike Duke

Input: a. TPP of output of good Y for combinations of A and B
        b. average fixed cost for each output level: AFC
        c. average variable cost for each level of output: AVC
        d. average cost for each level of output: ATC
        e. marginal cost for each level of output: MC
        f. market price for good Y: P(Y)
        g. total revenue relationship: TR
        h. marginal revenue relationship: MR
        Note: Data for a. through e. originated in assignment 25.

Output: a. TPP of output of good Y for combinations of A and B
        b. total revenue for each output level: TR
        c. marginal revenue for each output level: MR

INPUT AREA:

TPP	AFC	AVC	ATC	MC	P(Y)	TR	MR
0					$60	=P(Y)*TPP	=$(TR_i-TR_{i-1})/(TPP_i-TPP_{i-1})$
10	$150.00	60.00	210.00	$60			
20	$75.00	55.00	130.00	$50			
30	$50.00	50.00	100.00	$40			
40	$37.50	45.00	82.50	$30			
50	$30.00	40.00	70.00	$20			
60	$25.00	38.33	63.33	$30			
70	$21.43	38.57	60.00	$40			
80	$18.75	41.25	60.00	$60			
90	$16.67	45.56	62.22	$80			
100	$15.00	52.00	67.00	$110			
110	$13.64	60.00	73.64	$140			
120	$12.50	72.50	85.00	$210			

OUTPUT AREA:

TPP	AFC	AVC	ATC	MC	TR	MR
0					$0	
10	$150.00	$60.00	$210.00	$60	$600	$60
20	$75.00	$55.00	$130.00	$50	$1,200	$60
30	$50.00	$50.00	$100.00	$40	$1,800	$60
40	$37.50	$45.00	$82.50	$30	$2,400	$60
50	$30.00	$40.00	$70.00	$20	$3,000	$60
60	$25.00	$38.33	$63.33	$30	$3,600	$60
70	$21.43	$38.57	$60.00	$40	$4,200	$60
80	$18.75	$41.25	$60.00	**$60**	$4,800	**$60**
90	$16.67	$45.56	$62.22	$80	$5,400	$60
100	$15.00	$52.00	$67.00	$110	$6,000	$60
110	$13.64	$60.00	$73.64	$140	$6,600	$60
120	$12.50	$72.50	$85.00	$210	$7,200	$60

26b. **Line chart**

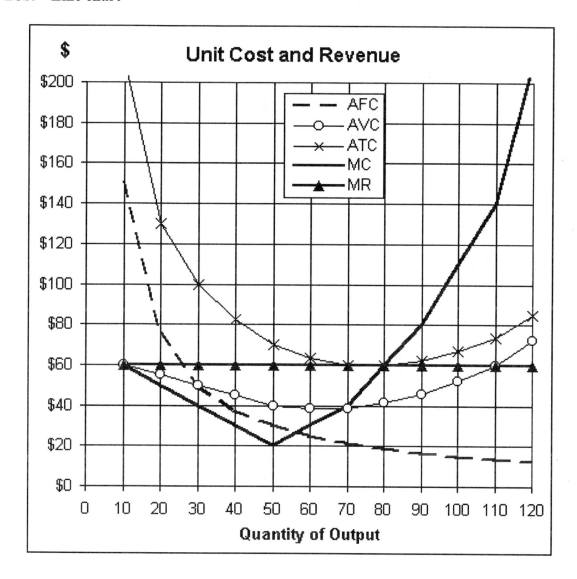

c. **What output would this firm choose to produce and how would this output be determined?**

Answer: The firm would choose to produce 80 units of Y. It would produce all units where MR≥MC because these units add more to total revenue than to total costs. Thus, the result would be the maximum profit or minimum loss output.

d. **WHAT IF the price of good Y (P(Y)) increased to $80. Put this data into the worksheet and determine the firm's optimum output.**

Answer: At a price of $80, output would be 90 units.

30. PROFIT ANALYSIS
a. Worksheet (File ID and Input Area)

FILE IDENTIFICATION AREA
Filename: Profit Analysis # 30
Designer: Mike Duke
Input: a. TPP of output of good Y for combinations of good A and B
          b. total revenue for each output level: TR
          c. total cost for each level of output: TC
          d. marginal revenue for each output level: MR
          e. marginal cost for each level of output: MC
          f. profit relationship: Profit
          Note: Data for a, c, and e are taken from assignment 25
Output: a. TPP of output of good Y for combinations of good A and B
          b. total revenue for each output level: TR
          c. total cost for each level of output: TC
          d. profit at each level of output: Profit
          e. marginal revenue for each output level: MR
          f. marginal cost at each level of output: MC
File Created:
File Modified:
File Last Used:

INPUT AREA:

TPP	TR	TC	MR	MC	Profit
0	$0	$1,500			=TR-TC
10	$600	$2,100	$60	$60	
20	$1,200	$2,600	$60	$50	
30	$1,800	$3,000	$60	$40	
40	$2,400	$3,300	$60	$30	
50	$3,000	$3,500	$60	$20	
60	$3,600	$3,800	$60	$30	
70	$4,200	$4,200	$60	$40	
80	$4,800	$4,800	$60	$60	
90	$5,400	$5,600	$60	$80	
100	$6,000	$6,700	$60	$110	
110	$6,600	$8,100	$60	$140	
120	$7,200	$10,200	$60	$210	

30a. Worksheet (Output Area)

OUTPUT AREA:

TPP	TR	TC	Profit	MR	MC	MR-MC
0	$0	1,500	-$1,500			
10	$600	2,100	-$1,500	$60	$60	$0
20	$1,200	2,600	-$1,400	$60	$50	$10
30	$1,800	3,000	-$1,200	$60	$40	$20
40	$2,400	3,300	-$900	$60	$30	$30
50	$3,000	3,500	-$500	$60	$20	$40
60	$3,600	3,800	-$200	$60	$30	$30
70	$4,200	4,200	$0	$60	$40	$20
80	$4,800	4,800	**$0**	**$60**	**$60**	**$0**
90	$5,400	5,600	-$200	$60	$80	-$20
100	$6,000	6,700	-$700	$60	$110	-$50
110	$6,600	8,100	-$1,500	$60	$140	-$80
120	$7,200	10,200	-$3,000	$60	$210	-$150

b. **What is the maximum profit? What does that mean?**
Answer: The maximum profit is $0. This means that the best this firm can do at a price of $60 for good Y is to produce where TR is equal to TC. However, since normal profit is included in total costs as an implicit opportunity cost, this firm is making a normal profit.

How much output will this firm produce seeking to maximize its profit or minimize its losses? How was this quantity determined?
Answer: This firm will produce 80 units of Y. The firm will produce all units that add more to total revenue than it adds to total cost, or if MR >MC. It will stop when it reaches the point where MR=MC since it has produced all units that benefit its profit or minimize its loss.

30c. **Line charts**

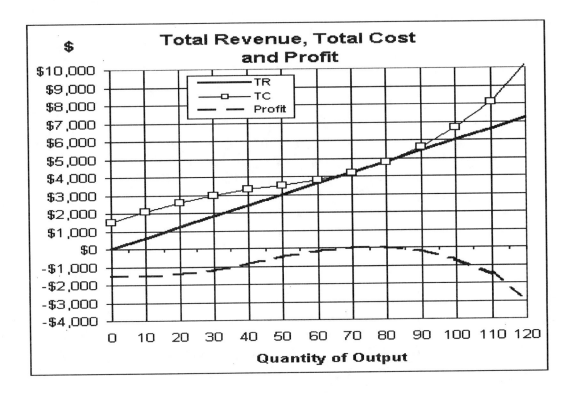

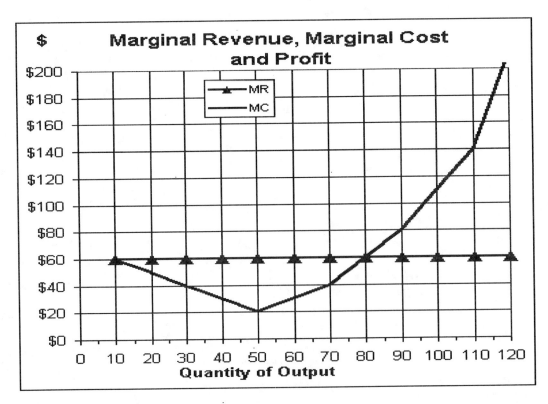

30d. **Explain how these charts show the same optimum (profit maximizing or loss minimizing) output level.**

Answer: In the first chart (TR/TC/profit), at a quantity of 80 the TR and TC curves are tangent showing zero economic profit. The profit curve reaches zero as well. At all other outputs, TC is greater than TR so profit is negative (or the firm is making losses).

In the second chart (MR and MC) at all outputs less than 80, additional units add more to revenue than to cost (MR>MC). At 80 units, MR=MC. At outputs greater than 80, the additional units add more to costs than to revenue (MC>MR).

e. **WHAT IF the market price for good Y increases to $80. Put this data into the worksheet and determine the firm's optimum output and profit or loss.**

Answer: At a price of $80, output rises to 90 units. The firm makes an economic profit of $2600. (TR = $80*90 = $7200. TC = $5600)

35. SHORT RUN SUPPLY FOR THE PERFECT COMPETITOR
a. Worksheet (File ID and Input Area)

FILE IDENTIFICATION AREA
Filename: Short Run Supply for the Perfect Competitor # 35
Designer: Mike Duke
Input Required:
      a. total physical product showing output of good Y for combinations
          of good A and B: TPP
      b. average variable cost for each level of output: AVC
      c. average cost for each level of output: ATC
      d. marginal cost for each level of output: MC
      e. possible market prices for good Y: P(Y)
      f. the marginal/average revenue relationship based on market price: MR/AR
      Note: Data for a. through d. are taken from assignment 25.
Output :
      a. total physical product of output of good Y for combinations
          of good A and B: TPP
      b. average variable cost for each level of output: AVC
      c. average cost for each level of output: ATC
      d. marginal cost for each level of output: MC
      e. marginal revenue each level of outputfor each of the specified
          market prices: MR1, MR2, MR3 and MR4

File Created:
File Modified:
File Last Used:

INPUT AREA:

TPP	AVC	ATC	MC	P(Y)	MR (or AR)
0				$30	=P(Y)
10	$60.00	$210.00	$60	$40	
20	$55.00	$130.00	$50	$60	
30	$50.00	$100.00	$40	$80	
40	$45.00	$82.50	$30		
50	$40.00	$70.00	$20		
60	$38.33	$63.33	$30		
70	$38.57	$60.00	$40		
80	$41.25	$60.00	$60		
90	$45.56	$62.22	$80		
100	$52.00	$67.00	$110		
110	$60.00	$73.64	$140		
120	$72.50	$85.00	$210		

35a. Worksheet (Output Area)

OUTPUT AREA:

TPP	AVC	ATC	MC	MR₁	MR₂	MR₃	MR₄
0							
10	$60.00	$210.00	$60	$30	$40	$60	$80
20	$55.00	$130.00	$50	$30	$40	$60	$80
30	$50.00	$100.00	$40	$30	$40	$60	$80
40	$45.00	$82.50	$30	$30	$40	$60	$80
50	$40.00	$70.00	$20	$30	$40	$60	$80
60	$38.33	$63.33	$30	$30	$40	$60	$80
70	$38.57	$60.00	**$40**	$30	**$40**	$60	$80
80	$41.25	$60.00	**$60**	$30	$40	**$60**	$80
90	$45.56	$62.22	**$80**	$30	$40	$60	**$80**
100	$52.00	$67.00	$110	$30	$40	$60	$80
110	$60.00	$73.64	$140	$30	$40	$60	$80
120	$72.50	$85.00	$210	$30	$40	$60	$80

c. Line chart

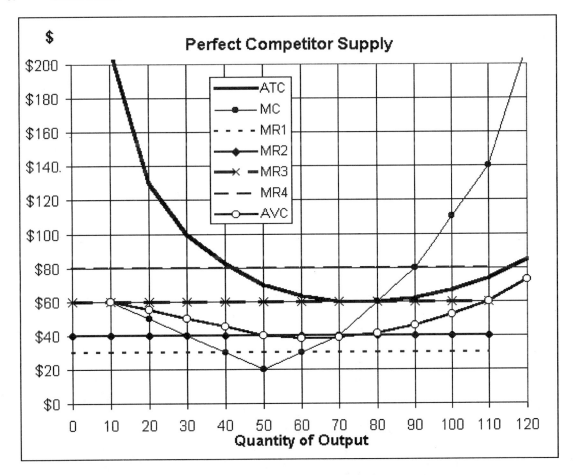

35 c. **A firm will seek to maximize its profit (or minimize its loss) by producing output where marginal revenue is equal to marginal cost (MR=MC). If marginal revenue is $30, what output will the firm produce?**

Answer: The firm will shut down and not produce output at any marginal revenue value less than average variable cost. The reason is that if it produces output, the revenue it receives at that market price will not even cover the variable factor costs. If it shuts down, its losses will be limited to only its fixed costs.

d. **What part of the perfectly competitive firms' marginal cost curve represents its short run supply curve?**

Answer: The portion of the marginal cost curve above the minimum point of the average variable cost curve.

44. MONOPOLIST PROFIT
a. Worksheet (File ID and Input Area)

FILE IDENTIFICATION AREA
Filename: Profit for the Monopolist # 44
Designer: Mike Duke
Input Required:

       a. quantity of output (TPP): Q
       b. average variable cost for each level of output: AVC
       c. average cost for each level of output: ATC
       d. marginal cost for each level of output: MC
       e. total revenue relationship: TR
       f. average revenue relationship (demand expressed as price
              being a function of quantity, P(Qd)): AR
       g. marginal revenue relationship: MR
       h. profit relationship: Profit
       Note: Data for a. through d. are taken from assignment 25.

Output :

       a. quantity of output (TPP): Q
       b. average variable cost for each level of output: AVC
       c. average cost for each level of output: ATC
       d. marginal cost for each level of output: MC
       e. total revenue for each level of output: TR
       f. average revenue for each level of output: AR
       g. marginal revenue each level of output: MR

       h. profit (or loss) for each level of output: Profit

File Created:
File Modified:
File Last Used:

INPUT AREA:

Q	AVC	ATC	MC	TR	AR	MR	Profit
0				=PQ or	=118-.8*Q	=(TR$_i$-TR$_{i-1}$)/(Q$_i$-Q$_{i-1}$)	=(AR-ATC)*Q
10	$60.00	$210.00	$60	=AR*Q			or =TR-TC
20	$55.00	$130.00	$50				
30	$50.00	$100.00	$40				
40	$45.00	$82.50	$30				
50	$40.00	$70.00	$20				
60	$38.33	$63.33	$30				
70	$38.57	$60.00	$40				
80	$41.25	$60.00	$60				
90	$45.56	$62.22	$80				
100	$52.00	$67.00	$110				
110	$60.00	$73.64	$140				
120	$72.50	$85.00	$210				

44a. Worksheet (Output Area)

OUTPUT AREA:

Q	AVC	ATC	MC	TR	AR	MR	Profit
0				$0			
10	$60.00	$210.00	$60	$1,100	$110	$110	-$1,000
20	$55.00	$130.00	$50	$2,040	$102	$94	-$560
30	$50.00	$100.00	$40	$2,820	$94	$78	-$180
40	$45.00	$82.50	$30	$3,440	$86	$62	$140
50	$40.00	$70.00	$20	$3,900	$78	$46	$400.00
60	**$38.33**	**$63.33**	**$30**	**$4,200**	**$70**	**$30**	**$400.20**
70	$38.57	$60.00	$40	$4,340	$62	$14	$140.00
80	$41.25	$60.00	$60	$4,320	$54	-$2	-$480.00
90	$45.56	$62.22	$80	$4,140	$46	-$18	-$1,460
100	$52.00	$67.00	$110	$3,800	$38	-$34	-$2,900
110	$60.00	$73.64	$140	$3,300	$30	-$50	-$4,800
120	$72.50	$85.00	$210	$2,640	$22	-$66	-$7,560

b.   **Using marginal analysis, what rule and level of output would this firm choose to produce in order to maximize its profit (or minimize its short-run losses)?**
Answer: The firm would produce at a quantity of 60 units where MR=MC.

44c. **Line chart**

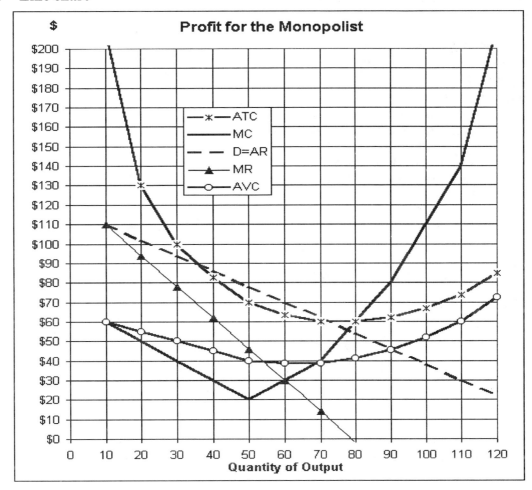

d. **Using the chart, determine the level of output the firm should produce in order to maximize its profit and the price it could sell the good for. Explain how you used the chart to determine these values.**
Answer: Quantity would be 60 at the intersection of the MR and MC curves. Market price for 60 units would be about $70 as determined by the market demand/average revenue curve (D=AR).

e. **Is the firm making a profit or loss? Explain your answer by using the chart.**
Answer: The firm is making a profit. At 60 units of output (where MR=MC) the AR curve is above the ATC.
Using the data for profit that was calculated, determine how much profit this firm will be making. Answer: $400.20 at an output of 60
What would happen to the optimum output and profit if the market demand curve shifted to the left? Answer: The optimum output would fall and profits would fall or even become short-run losses.

51. PRESENT VALUE

a. Worksheet

FILE IDENTIFICATION AREA
Filename: Present Value # 51
Designer: Mike Duke
Input Required:
        a. amount of net future payment: FV
        b. discount rate or market interest rate: r
        c. number of interest time periods: n
        d. present value relationship: PV
Output: present value of a future payment: PV
INPUT AREA:

FV	r	n	PV
$1,000.00	0.05	1	$=FV/(1+r)^n$
$1,000.00	0.05	10	
$1,000.00	0.1	1	
$1,000.00	0.1	10	

OUTPUT AREA:

PV_1:	$952.38
PV_2:	$613.91
PV_3:	$909.09
PV_4:	$385.54

b. **Comparing PV_1 to PV_3, what is the effect on present value of a higher discount or interest rate? Explain why this makes sense.**
Answer: Present value is lower the higher the discount rate. The higher the prevailing interest rate, the smaller the amount needed in the present to grow it to the future payment.

c. **Comparing PV_2 to PV_1, what is the effect of a future payment being payable farther in the future on its present value? Explain why this makes sense.**
Answer: The farther into the future the amount is payable, the smaller its present value. The longer a future payment is payable in the future, the smaller a present amount would be needed in order to grow it to the future value because the interest will have a longer time to accumulate and to compound.

d. **Comparing PV_1 to PV_3 and PV_2 to PV_4, what happens to the difference between present values at different interest rates the longer the term until the future payment is due? What causes this effect?**
Answer: The longer the term until the future payment is due, the greater the difference between the present value at a lower interest rate and at a higher interest rate. This occurs due to the compounding of interest over longer periods of time.

54. PRODUCTION POSSIBILITY FRONTIER (CURVE)
a. Worksheet

FILE IDENTIFICATION AREA
Filename: Production Possibility Frontier # 54
Designer: Mike Duke
Input Required:
  a. quantity of good A (software): Q(A)
  b. quantity of good B (food): Q(B)
Output :
  a. quantity of good A : Q(A)
  b. quantity of good B: Q(B)
File Created:
File Modified:
File Last Used:

INPUT AREA:

Q(A)	Q(B)
0	44,000
4,000	43,500
8,000	43,000
12,000	42,000
16,000	41,000
20,000	39,000
24,000	35,500
28,000	32,000
32,000	27,000
36,000	21,000
40,000	14,000
44,000	0

OUTPUT AREA:

Q(A)	Q(B)
0	44,000
4,000	43,500
8,000	43,000
12,000	42,000
16,000	41,000
20,000	39,000
24,000	35,500
28,000	32,000
32,000	27,000
36,000	21,000
40,000	14,000
44,000	0

54b. **Line chart**

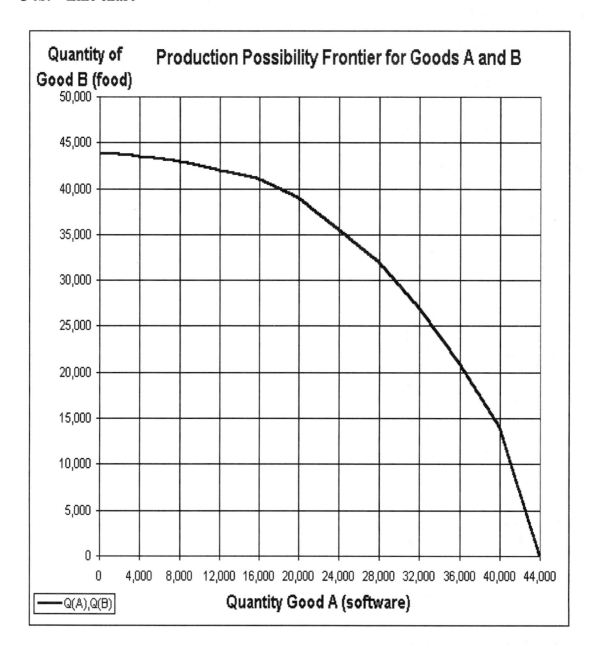

59.   IMPACT OF AN IMPORT QUOTA

a.   Worksheet

FILE IDENTIFICATION
AREA
Filename: Impact of an Import Quota # 59
Designer: Mike Duke
Input Required:

a. quantity: Q

b. demand relationship expressed as price being a function of quantity: P(Qd)

c. supply relationship expressed as price being a function of quantity: P(Qs)

d. supply from the world market (perfectly elastic supply at the world price): Pw

e. quota (limit on number of units that can be imported): Qim

f. supply relationship with quota at world price or above: P(Qs+Qim)

Output: Supply and Demand Schedules

a. quantity: (Q)

b. price at each quantity demanded: P(Qd)

c. price at each quantity supplied: P(Qs)

d. world supply: Pw

e. supply with import quota at each quantity supplied at world price or above: P(Qs+Qim)

File Created:
File Modified:

INPUT AREA:

Q	P(Qd)	P(Qs)	Pw	Qim	P(Qs+Qim)
0	=55-.5*Qd	=5+.5*Qs	$20	20	=-5+.5*Qs or
10					=5+.5*Qs-.5*Qim
20					
30					
40					
50					
60					
70					
80					
90					
100					

OUTPUT AREA:

Q	P(Qd)	P(Qs)	Pw	P(Qs+Qim)
0	$55.00	$5.00	$20	
10	$50.00	$10.00	$20	
20	$45.00	$15.00	$20	
30	$40.00	$20.00	$20	
40	$35.00	$25.00	$20	
50	**$30.00**	**$30.00**	$20	$20.00
60	**$25.00**	$35.00	$20	**$25.00**
70	**$20.00**	$40.00	**$20**	$30.00
80	$15.00	$45.00	$20	$35.00
90	$10.00	$50.00	$20	$40.00
100	$5.00	$55.00	$20	$45.00

59b.   Line chart

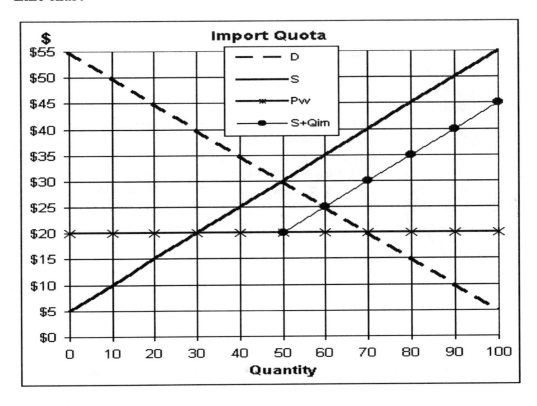

c.   **Referring to the line chart, if there were not an import quota what would the equilibrium price and quantity be?**
Answer: Equilibrium price would be $20 at a quantity of 70.
With the quota of 20, what is the equilibrium price and quantity?
Answer: Price is $25 and quantity is 60. When price is $25, the quantity demanded (D) is equal to the quantity supplied plus the quota (S+Qim).

d.   **Referring to the line chart, when an import quota is imposed, what happens to producers surplus in the importing country? Why?**
Answer: Producer surplus increases because the domestic producers now receive a higher price ($25 rather than $20, the world price) and they sell more units of output (40 rather than 30 units).

e.   **What happens to consumer surplus in the importing country as a result of the quota? Why?**
Answer: Consumer surplus decreases because consumers will be paying a higher price ($25 rather than $20) and purchasing a smaller quantity (60 rather than 70 units).
Which is larger, the gain in domestic producer surplus or the loss of domestic consumer surplus? Answer: The consumer surplus loss is greater.

65. COMPARATIVE ADVANTAGE

a. Worksheet

FILE IDENTIFICATION
AREA
Filename: Comparative Advantage # 65
Designer: Mike Duke
Input Required:

    a. quantity of good A (hair cuts) for Rene in 8 hours: QAr

    b. quantity of good B (shampoos) for Rene in 8 hours: QBr

    c. quantity of good A for Jean in 8 hours: QAj

    d. quantity of good B for Jean in 8 hours: QBj

    e. Rene's quantity of good A linear relationship in terms of good B: QAr(QB)

    f. Jene's quantity of good A for linear relationship in terms of good B: QAj(QB)

    g. total quantity of good A relationship when each spends an equal proportion
        of time on good B: QAr(QB)+QAj(QB)

    h. exchange relationship of good A for good B in trade: QA(QB)

Output : a. quantities of good B that Rene and Jean produce together in 8 hours: QB

    b. quantity of good A for Rene for each quantity of good B: QAr(QB)

    c. quantity of good A for Jean for each quantity of good B: QAj(QB)

    d. total quantity of good A when each spends an equal proportion of time on
        good B: QAr(QB)+QAj(QB)

    e. total quantity of good A when each specializes in their the lowest
        opportunity cost good: QArj(QB)

    f. quantity of good A traded for each quantity of good B exchanged: QA(QB)

INPUT AREA:

Qar	QBr	Qaj	QBj	QAr(QB)	QAj(QB)	QAr(QB)+QAj(QB)	QA(QB)
10	20	20	10	=10-.5*QB	=20-2*QB	=30-QB	=20-QB

OUTPUT AREA:

QB	QAr(QB)	QAj(QB)	QAr(QB)+QAj(QB)	QArj(QB)	QA(QB)
0	10.0	20.0	30	30.0	20
2	9.0	16.0	28	29.0	18
4	8.0	12.0	26	28.0	16
6	7.0	8.0	24	27.0	14
8	6.0	4.0	22	26.0	12
10	5.0	0.0	20	25.0	10
12	4.0		18	24.0	8
14	3.0		16	23.0	6
16	2.0		14	22.0	4
18	1.0		12	21.0	2
20	0.0		10	20.0	0
22			8	16.0	
24			6	12.0	
26			4	8.0	
28			2	4.0	
30			0	0.0	

65b. **Determine which individual has the lowest opportunity cost (gives up the least amount of the other good for each unit produced) for good A and who has the lowest opportunity cost for good B. Assuming they try to specialize in what they have comparative advantage in, determine how much of good A they will produce at each quantity B (QB) point. Label this QArj(QB). From QB=0 to QB=20, Rene will be producing all of the good B specified at each point while Jean produces only good A. Why?**

Answer: Rene's opportunity cost of producing good B is only one-half unit of good A, but Jean's is 2 units of good A. They will produce larger combinations of good A and good B if Jean specialized in good A and Rene produces the good B at each quantity point up to 20 (that is all of good B that Rene can produce).

From the good B quantity point of 20 to 30, Jean will have to produce the additional good B. What happens to the trade off in terms of the reduction good A produced in order to increase good B production?

Answer: The trade off becomes four times as great. That is, each unit of good B produced by Jean reduces good A by two units rather than one-half unit as was the case when good B was being increased by Rene; thus reducing the production of good A by a larger amount for each unit of good B provided.

c. **Line chart**

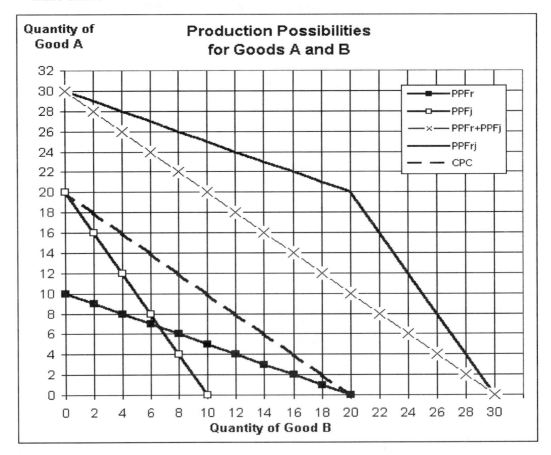

65d. **Comparing PPFr+PPFj to PPFrj, what is occurring in terms of the joint production with and without specialization in accordance with comparative advantage?**

Answer: The joint production with specialization (PPFrj) contains greater combinations of good A and B than their non-specialized joint production (PPFr+PPFj), except at the end points where both are producing only one good and specialization is not possible.

What is the incentive for Rene and Jean to specialize in accordance with comparative advantage?

Answer: The incentive is more output from the same resources leading to higher income for each.

e. **If Rene and Jean traded doing the shampoos or hair cuts for each other's customers in accordance with comparative advantage, what would the CPC demonstrate about the number of each type of good they would be paid for?**

Answer: The CPC would demonstrate what they could be paid for in terms of haircuts and shampoos in eight hours whereas their own PPFs would show only what they could do and be paid for by themselves.

Index

A
absolute addressing, 11
autofill, 26
autofilter, 28
automatic sums, 13

C
cell, 5
centering, 9
central processing unit (CPU), 1
charts, 20
closing files, 3
column chart, 24
column width, 9
comma icon, 16
computer components, 1
control panel, 5
copy and paste, 10
copying formulas, 10
"currency style" icon, 16

D
data form, 26
data sort, 27
database, 26
delete row or column, 8

E
editing cells, 7
editing worksheet, 5
exiting, 4

F
fields,26
file ID, 29
format axis menu box, 23
formatting
    customized, 16
    numbers, 15
formulas, 10
freeze panes, 14
functions, 17
    date and time, 19
    financial, 19
    math and trig, 19
    statistical, 19

I
icon, 3
importing data, 15
input area, 30
inserting rows and column, 7
input alignment, 30

L
line chart, 20

M
main memory, 1
manual recalculation, 30
"merge and center" icon, 9
moving cell contents, 7

N
numeric formats, list of, 17

O
operating systems software, 2

P
paste special, 10
payment calculations, 17
"percentage" icon, 16
pie chart, 24
printing, 4

R
random access memory (RAM), 1
read only memory (ROM), 1
records, 26
relative addressing, 11
retrieving (opening) a file, 3
rows and columns,5
   inserting, 7
row width, 9

S
saving files, 3
series tab, 21
shifting cells, 8
sorting, 13

W
Windows, 3
Worksheet, 5
   Requirements, 29